SELECTED POEMS AND TRANSLATIONS
1969–1991

Selected Poems
and Translations

1969–1991

WILLIAM MATTHEWS

Houghton Mifflin Company

Boston   New York   London

1992

Library of Congress Cataloging-in-Publication Data

Matthews, William, date.
  [Selections. 1992]
  Selected poems and translations, 1969–1991 / William
    p.   cm.
  Includes index.
  ISBN 0-395-63121-1
  I. Title
PS3563.A855A6 1992   91-45716
811'.54 — DC20   CIP

Printed in the United States of America

HAD   10 9 8 7 6 5 4 3 2 1

FOR PAT

Contents

Selected Translations from Martial

from *Foreseeable Futures* (1987)

Selected Translations from the Bulgarian (1991)

from *Blues If You Want* (1989)

from

Ruining the New Road

(1970)

THE SEARCH PARTY

I wondered if the others felt
as heroic
and as safe: *my* unmangled family
slept while I slid uncertain feet ahead
behind my flashlight's beam.
Stones, thick roots as twisted as
a ruined body,
what did I fear?
I hoped my batteries
had eight more lives
than the lost child.
I feared I'd find something.

Reader, by now you must be sure
you know just where we are,
deep in symbolic woods.
Irony, self-accusation,
someone else's suffering.
The search is that of art.

You're wrong, though it's
an intelligent mistake.
There was a real lost child.
I don't want to swaddle it
in metaphor.
I'm just a journalist
who can't believe in objectivity.
I'm in these poems
because I'm in my life.
But I digress.

A man four volunteers
to the left of me
made the discovery.

We circled in like waves
returning to the parent shock.
You've read this far, you might as well
have been there too. Your eyes accuse
me of false chase. Come off it,
you're the one who thought it wouldn't
matter what we found.
Though we came with lights
and tongues thick in our heads,
the issue was a human life.
The child was still
alive. Admit you're glad.

BLUES FOR JOHN COLTRANE, DEAD AT 41

Although my house floats on a lawn
as plush as a starlet's body
and my sons sleep easily,
I think of death's salmon breath
leaping back up the saxophone
with its wet kiss.

Hearing him dead,
I feel it in my feet
as if the house were rocked
by waves from a soundless speedboat
planing by, full throttle.

LUST

It is a squad car idling
through my eyes, bored,
looking for a crime to crush.
Two tough cops drive it,
three years on the same beat,
sick of each other.
To it I am no better
than a radish.
I hear its indolent engine
grump along in second gear,
feel both cops watch me
walk with stiff ankles,
a nun among drunks.

MOVING

When we spurt off
in the invalid Volvo
flying its pennant of blue fumes,
the neighbors group and watch.
We twist away like a released balloon.

SCHOOL

Who was the last English king
to die by violence?
Hands clamor, Let me Let me
kill Charles I.
I bring my tongue down hard.
We gleam, our eyes the color
of the robes the saved put on.
We know everything.

Why We Are Truly a Nation

Because we rage inside
the old boundaries,
like a young girl leaving the Church,
scared of her parents.

Because we all dream of saving
the shaggy, dung-caked buffalo,
shielding the herd with our bodies.

Because grief unites us,
like the locked antlers of moose
who die on their knees in pairs.

What You Need

Suppose you want to leave your life,
that old ring in the tub,
behind?

It closes cozily
as a clerk's hand,
a coin with fingers.

You hate it
the same way the drunken son
loves Mother.

You will need pain
heaving under you
like frost ruining the new road.

WEHLENER SONNENUHR AUSLESE 1959

for Dave Curry

After each rain the workers
bring the eroded soil
back up the slope in baskets.
When the freezing ground heaves
rocks up, they are gathered,
shattered, the pieces
strewn among the vines.
The sun reflects from them.
In the Moselle the sun
is a broken bottle of light,
same color as the wine.
When you drink it,
you pass through your body
a beloved piece of earth.
You are like the worm,
except you know it.
A door in the earth opens
and you go in, as guest.

ON CAPE COD A CHILD IS STOLEN

Fog has sealed in the house
like a ship in a bottle.
All the people of the house
are dreaming of his future;
only the Puritans
and he aren't sleeping.
They watch him lie too long in bed,
the fog's moist nose at his ear.
Now the muzzle pokes his tiny mouth,
prying it open. They love him;
he's in danger; but it's too late.

His perfect body is still there
but clearly empty. The fog
rolls back to its own place
and the fishermen scrape back
from breakfast and go out to work.

Poems Not Collected in Book Form

March Heat

At night the wind dies
like a settling canvas.

Under a clotted sky
complaints swarm at great distances,
their slow wings beating.

From their windows
tenants lean out,
ladling the thick air in.

Nothing can ease the March heat
nor make it stay.

The Cloud

Here I am again,
fleet and green —
something that has left the shrubs
bleached, but in the old shapes,
some vegetable force
noticed only by its absence —
malingering through the house.

I rub my back on the ceiling
like smoke from the crushed cigarette
of a lover
escaped just in time:

the husband is coming
downstairs: a tennis ball,
a one-drop waterfall.
He has been wakened
from dreaming of love.

I hide in the shower.
This is fun! This is better
than rocking like a chair
someone has leapt up from,
rocking on my knees,
a nauseous monk,
the body shaken and sick
from dreaming of love,

my mind a thicket I peer from
watching my body vomit —
every nerve, every cilium
flapping free of its snapped tether.
I am a little fist
of shower mist,
a snarl in the dank air.

When it is safe I come out,
pale, bereft.
I want to tarnish the silverware,
to sleep in a drawer
forever, a tacky gift
dreaming of love.

I want to grow on the mirrors —
a mossy breath,
a life without a body
shaken and sick,
a life no larger than the smear
of structured slime, the microbe
that will kill me
dreaming of love.

I'm going to send you this poem
when I've finished it, it will
embarrass you
dreaming of love,
of the beach from which the cloud parade
is always starting
outward.
If the dream is inland,
the beach is a bed,
your body shaken and sick
of its dreaming of love,
the pale men stepping off the side
like suicidal pillows.
They have taken the wrong turn
for the Temple.
Perhaps you gave the directions,
dreaming of love,
your body shaken and sick
of its pale flags
nobody could see in a mist?
Where is the cloud flotilla?
It is carrying food to the fat ones.

Meanwhile in the kitchen
my tryst with the teakettle
had failed.
I'm oozing upstairs, I'm
like a beer growing a smaller head.
Here on this bed
I've dreamed of the love of one woman
at a time,
not caring whom.
My body curled to sleep, a statue
of a snake.
There are no straight lines in nature.
If I writhed,
chances are
I was dreaming of love.

Then I would wake
to the trill in the forsythia,
the birds blunt in their needs.
Nothing in nature repeats.

So I rose —
a new noise
from a dropped tambourine.
And then I went to bed some more
and here I am
floating above my body,
a threatening rain
dreaming of love.

Who wants to hover long?
Those pale plants are my fault.
The ground is to fall down on
dreaming of love,
the body shaken and sick.

Wherever you are
dreaming of love,
good night.
The ferns of blood and light
knit shut my eyes,
coals in a later life.
Ashes to ashes, breath to breath.

Then I will go
down for breakfast
in a substantial dew.
Shredded wheat!
This must be how the medium feels
when his astral body comes
home after the seance —
foolish, whole.
Perhaps I am a fraud
dreaming of love,
my body shaken and sick.

The cold milk beads its glass.
The shrubs gleam green.
Dust in the lit air swirls.
I broke from my bed
like a pheasant.
I'm leaving myself off the hook
all day, you'll have to come over.
This is like the light before a tornado,
and it is only a new morning —
the ravelled wheat reknit in its bowl,
the milk staring
from its faceted glass like a white bee,
the smooth udder of the sun
hung over my head
and yours, wherever you are.
I feel like a new tree,
a cloud with a stem
sunk in the earth of the body's
dream about the body
shaken and sick
dreaming of love.

ETERNALLY UNDISMAYED ARE THE POOLSHOOTERS

for Robert Peterson

A slow circular flail of fan
not moving the still air.
Shee-it. Slap of pool balls. Hot.
Arms sag from sweat-stained sockets,
drenched tendrils.

"It's so hot at my place
you can hear the paint crack."

Everything's slick with a soft sweaty grit.
In the parking lot
a sponge-tongued beagle

spurns a dirty puddle
shaped like a woman's foot,
crumples into the shade
beneath a Buick, sleeps.

She loved heat.
On the beach for hours
like a snake, then daintily
to the water, foamtoes,
one deep breast-heaving breath
and in.

"104 out there. Too hot to fuck.
I once loved a woman left me
on a day like this."
We woke marbled with sweat.
"Those days I was working straight commission,
I could sell a truss to a trout.
I said, my love
let's buy an air conditioner.
She put my shirt on, then her slacks."
Like a bride aiming her bouquet
at a tubby friend, she tossed me
her underpants and left.
"I haven't seen her since."

Each ball slides for no reason
where it wants,
glasses of beer warm up to room
temperature (about 78°)
at the same pace
the balls click quietly
like tumblers in a lock.
Freddie brings the paper in,
hangs around, goes back out.

Nothing from the poolshooters,
faces of camels
working their gums
among the smoke rings.

THIS SPUD'S FOR YOU

1.

Of *solanum tuberosum*, that vagrant vegetable,
the Odysseus of tubers, the lumpy pill of the poor
and starving, the shape-shifting and soothing potato,
I sing. For all the long years it lay locked
in the cool vault of the Andes, above 11,000
feet, where maize won't grow, where the Indians
ate the fattest and best and planted the runts,
so that when the first Europeans held one
it was but a starchy pebble, the Indians
no doubt had a potato song, but the Europeans
brought back to those who had hoped for gold
a mute, misshapen, marble-sized seed crop
and it was reviled. How many times have we met
the news that would save us with contumely?
Thus did Europe greet the immigrant potato
Not mentioned in the Bible, cousin to nightshade,
it was *flatulent and indigestible . . . , pasty
and naturally insipid; it might prove good to swine.*
It was *an Egyptian fruit whose cultivation
may possibly have some value in the colonies,*
and it was a lurch on the path to hell,
according to Nietzsche: *A diet which consists
predominantly of rice leads to the use of opium,
just as a diet which consists predominantly
of potatoes leads to the use of liquor.*
It was *Ireland's lazy root,* and it ruined
Irish cuisine: *Bread is scarcely ever seen,
and the oven is unknown.* It was, in short,

the durable food of the poor and swarthy,
the bread of vegetables, not scarce, a stay
against famine, bland, despised by the rich.
But in Saxony and Westphalia, 1640,
when all the earth around lay acrid
from twenty-three of the Thirty Years
War, when human and animal corpses lay
swarming with worms, gnawed by birds,
wolves and dogs, for there was nobody
to bury them, pity them or weep for them,
Spanish soldiers arrived with a few potatoes.
When they gave potatoes to the peasants,
these unfortunates began by eating them
just as they were. A little later they planted them.

2.

I sing of Pedro de Cieza de Leon, one
of Pizarro's men, who first among Europeans
sang our rustic root crop in his *Chronicle*
of Peru (1553). And of Sir Francis Drake,
who took unknowingly on board at Cartagena,
in 1586, a few potatoes, and later took on board
in Virginia one Thomas Hariot, who noticed them,
and gave some to John Gerard (his famous *Herball*,
1597, thus misnamed "the Virginia potato").
Did Hariot give some to his boss, Sir Walter
Raleigh, who may then have become first
to plant them in Ireland, on his land
at Youghal, near Cork, late in 1586?
Did Raleigh make a gift to Queen Elizabeth
of some potatoes, and did the befuddled
royal cook discard the tuber and serve
the leaves, tasting like nasty cress?
Of what I do not know I do not sing,
for I have seen what foolish things
many a famous man and fancy writer said
about the potato, and am chastened.

3.
Thus I do not sing Antoine Augustin
Parmentier, the publicist of the potato,
a military pharmacist and pamphleteer,
hero of much Gallic potato lore,
almost all of it wrong, for he did not
charm Marie Antoinette by twining
potato flowers in her hair, nor give
Louis XVI potato flowers for his birthday
(August 23 — those would have been wan blooms),
nor did he serve to Benjamin Franklin
a meal in which every course was concocted
from potatoes, though he probably
presided over a like feast once at least.
The tireless potato flak was born to hustle,
that's all, and thus odds were he'd find
later in life a better project than
getting himself noticed by the great
with, as his dull escutcheon, the blunt
lumpy, uningratiating spud. Later
he introduced vaccination against smallpox
in the army, and today his name survives
attached to a soup, a hash and an omelet.

4.
I sing the canny potato, already buried
and thus not burned or trampled by invading
armies. The submarine of the loam,
it bears silently its cargo of carbohydrates
while soldiers and hunters of grouse
and tax assessors conduct important
business overhead. No wonder the poor
love the obdurate tuber, for they share
with it many a survival skill and enemy.
When the knell of the potato blight
rang and rang through starving Ireland,
the potato hunkered down, the lumpy *arriviste*,
blind as a thumb, soft cousin to the stone,

the mineral wealth of the Emerald Isle,
the dull, bland, satisfying food
that Brillat-Savarin proclaimed
only a protection against famine
(only?!), and it spent its three heroisms —
it waited, it grew a little, it flourished —
and the blight was defeated. The plump,
misshapen stowaway, the wily, lumpy
little *picaro*, the extender of stews
and thickener of soups, the sturdy,
reliable, ugly and invincible potato,
who would not sing this manna among tubers?
We have heard them quoted in this very poem,
and there may be others like them,
though perhaps they are not good singers,
and in any case, you and I, gentle readers,
we can lift our voices. All together now. . . .

from

Sleek for the Long Flight

(1972)

DRIVING ALONGSIDE THE HOUSATONIC RIVER ALONE ON A RAINY APRIL NIGHT

I remember asking
where does my shadow go at night?
I thought it went home,
it grew so sleek at dusk.
They said, you just don't
notice it, the way you don't tell yourself
how to walk or hear
a noise that doesn't stop.
But one wrong wobble
in the socket and inside the knee
chalk is falling, school
is over.
As if the ground were a rung
suddenly gone from a ladder,
the self, the shoulders bunched
against the road's each bump, the penis
with its stupid grin,
the whole rank slum of cells
collapses.
I feel the steering wheel
tug a little, testing.
For as long as that takes
the car is a sack of kittens
weighed down by stones.
The headlights chase a dark ripple
across some birch trunks.
I know it's there, water
hurrying over the shadow of water.

ANOTHER BEER

The first one was for the clock
and its one song
which is the song's name.

Then a beer for the scars in the table,
all healed in the shape of initials.

Then a beer for the thirst
and its one song we keep forgetting.

And a beer for the hands
we are keeping to ourselves.
The body's dogs, they lie
by the ashtray and thump
suddenly in their sleep.

And a beer for our reticence,
the true tongue, the one song,
the fire made of air.

Then a beer for the juke box.
I wish it had the recording
of a Marcel Marceau mime performance:
28 minutes of silence,
2 of applause.

And a beer for the phone booth.
In this confessional you can sit.
You sing it your one song.

And let's have a beer for whoever goes home
and sprawls, like the remaining sock,
in the drawer of his bed and repeats
the funny joke and pulls it
shut and sleeps.

And a beer for anyone
who can't tell the difference between
death and a good cry
with its one song.
None of us will rest enough.

The last beer is always for the road.
The road is what the car drinks
travelling on its tongue of light
all the way home.

THE CAT

While you read
the sleepmoth begins
to circle your eyes
and then —
a hail of claws
lands the cat
in your lap.
The little motor
in his throat
is how a cat says
Me. He rasps the soft
file of his tongue
along the inside
of your wrist.
He licks himself.
He's building
a pebble of fur
in his stomach.
And now he pulls
his body in a circle
around the fire of sleep.

This is the wet
sweater with legs
that shakes in
from the rain,
split-ear the sex burglar,
Fish-breath, Wind-
minion, paw-poker
of dust
tumbleweeds,
the cat that kisses
with the wet
flame of his tongue
each of your eyelids
as if sealing
a letter.

One afternoon
napping under the light-
ladder
let down by the window,
there are two of them:
cat and cat-
shadow, sleep.

One night you lay your book
down like the clothes
your mother wanted
you to wear tomorrow.
You yawn.
The cat exhales a moon.
Opening a moon,
you dream of cats.
One of them strokes you
the wrong way. Still,
you sleep well.

This is the same cat
Plunder.
This is the old cat

Milk-whiskers.
This is the cat
eating one of its lives.
This is the first cat
Fire-fur.
This is the next cat
St. Sorrow.
This is the cat with its claws
furled, like sleep's flag.
This is the lust cat
trying to sleep with its shadow.
This is the only cat
I have ever loved.
This cat has written
in tongue-ink
the poem you are reading now,
the poem scratching
at the gate of silence,
the poem
that forgives
itself
for its used-up lives,
the poem
of the cat waking,
running a long shudder
through his body,
stretching again,
following the moist bell
of his nose
into the world
again.

AND SO

you grow
in your cocoon of sleep,
like a dead sailor
revived inside his flag.

These memories of what
is about to happen, silences
the old dog Frostbite has just left. . . .
The tiny valleys of his pawprints —

so much like the black
empty lakes on dice —
fill with snow or moonlight
or some white thing or bone.

Remember the night the moon-
crescent was on its back
like a melon-rind or runner
of a rocking chair? The snow

seemed to be falling up,
smoke from silence's fire.
You watched as if your life
were being told in code.

Suppose you have an angel,
a shadow made of light
and reticence? Woman
be consoled by your strangeness, by

its ceremonies.
There's snow on the sandwiches.
Only a song you have never imagined
or the oil of the right harsh herb

can melt this meal of guilt
and stuttering intentions.
You begin a speech on
"pleasant pressures." It was

supposed to come out "present pleasures"
but never mind, already the snow is
in ascent and we're becoming food,
each body dark with hunger

to be eaten. We lie
down in the sandwiches.
The world is strange.
Look in our eyes and see.

NARCISSUS BLUES

> *Charity, come home,*
> *begin.*
> W. S. Merwin

When you rest your hands
on the table they rattle
like dice full of gamblers.
It's too long between feedings.
Then your wife is there, too,
begging for love, and while you explain
the soup gets dirty.
It's that damn gas heat
and she begins to snuffle
and calls you a toad
in a loud voice with the windows open.

It's as if you too could be
poor or insane
or need somebody
to hit, and your precise agonies
are nothing, and the brotherhood of pain
is spurious, and your tongue curls
like a harem slipper.

You're going to shave a stranger
backwards every morning
and not a word of thanks.

THE SNAKE

A snake is the love of a thumb
and forefinger.
Other times, an arm
that has swallowed a bicep.

The air behind this one
is like a knot
in a child's shoelace
come undone
while you were blinking.

It is bearing something away.
What? What time
does the next snake leave?

This one's tail is ravelling
into its burrow —
a rosary returned to a purse.
The snake is the last time your spine
could go anywhere alone.

from

Sticks & Stones

(1975)

THE PORTRAIT

Before the shutter blinks
the bored photographer can feel
the engaged couple stiffen —
lapse between a lightning-bolt
and thunder. It's easy.
A train of light streaks into the tunnel
of his lens and comes out
changed. He loves his darkroom
trance, air in an inky lung.
And in the hall
outside: bell-shaped, its lipped rim
pressed to the ceiling, a cream-
colored glass lampshade
is rung by ricocheting moths.

THE WASTE CARPET

No day is right for the apocalypse,
if you ask a housewife in Talking
Rock, Georgia, or maybe Hop River,
Connecticut. She is opening a plastic bag.
A grotesque parody of the primeval muck
starts oozing out. And behold,
the plastic bag is magic;
there is no closing it. Soap
in unsoftened water, sewage, asbestos
coiled like vermicelli, Masonite shavings,
a liquified lifetime subscription

to *The New York Times* delivered all at once.
Empty body stockings, limp, forlorn,
like collapsed lungs. A blithering slur
of face creams, an army of photocopies
travelling on its stomach of acronyms,
tooth paste tubes wrung rigid and dry.
Also, two hundred and one tons
of crumpled bumpers wrapped in insurance
claims, slag, coal dust, plastic trimmings,
industrial excrementa. Lake Erie is returning
our gifts.

At first she thought she had won
something. Now it slithers through the house,
out windows, down the street, spreading
everywhere but heading, mostly, west.
Maybe *heading* is the wrong word,
implying shape and choice. It took
the shape of the landscape
it rippled across like the last blanket.
And it went west because the way lay open
once again: not the same fecund rug
the earth grew when white people scraped
their first paths to the Pacific
across the waves of the inland grasses.

Outside Ravenswood, West Virginia,
abandoned cars shine in the sun
like beetlebacks. The ore it took
to make the iron it took to make the steel
it took to make the cars, that ore
would remember the glaciers if it could.
Now comes another grinding, but not —
thanks to our new techniques — so slow.
The amiable cars wait stilly in their pasture.
Three Edsels forage in the southeast corner
like bishops of a ruined church.
There are Fords and Dodges, a Mercury
on blocks, four Darts and a Pierce-Arrow,

a choir of silenced Chevrolets.
And, showing their lapsed trademarks
and proud grilles to a new westward
expansion, two Hudsons, a LaSalle
and a DeSoto.

    I was hoping to describe
the colors of this industrial autumn —
rust, a faded purple like the dusty
skin of a Concord grape, flaking moss-
green paint with primer peeking
blandly through, the garish macho reds
insurance companies punish, the greys
(opaque) and silvers (bright), the snob colors
(e.g., British Racing Green), the two-tone
combinations time will spurn like roadkill
(1957: pink and grey), cornflower
blue, naval blue, royal blue, stark blue, true
blue, the blacker blue the diver sees
beneath him when he plumbs thirty feet —
but now they are all covered,
rolling and churning in the last
accident, like bubbles in lava.

And now my Cincinnati — the hills
above the river, the lawn that drained
toward Richwood Ave. like a small valley of uncles,
the sultry river musk that slid
like a compromising note through my bedroom window —
and indeed all Cincinnati seethes. The vats
at Procter & Gamble cease their slick
congealing, and my beloved birthplace
is but another whorl of dirt.

Up north, near Lebanon and Troy and Rosewood,
the corn I skulked in as a boy
lies back its ears like a shamed dog.
Hair along the sow's spine rises.
The Holstein pivots his massive head

toward where the barn stood; the spreading stain
he sees is his new owner.

What we imagined was the fire-storm,
or, failing that, the glacier.
Or we hoped we'd get off easy,
losing only California.
With the seismologists and mystics
we saw the last California ridge
crumble into the ocean.

And we were ready with elegies:

O California, sportswear
and defense contracts, gasses that induce
deference, high school girls
with their own cars, we wanted
to love you without pain.

O California, when you were moored to us
like a vast splinter of melon,
like a huge and garish gondola,
then we were happier, although
we showed it by easy contempt.
But now you are lost at sea,
your cargo of mudslides and Chardonnays
lost, the prints of the old movies
lost, the thick unlighted candles of the redwoods
snuffed in advance. On the ocean floor
they lie like hands of a broken clock.

O California, here we come,
quoting Ecclesiastes,
ruinous with self-knowledge.

Meanwhile, because the muck won't stop
for lamentation, Kansas succumbs.
Drawn down by anklets of DDT,

the jayhawk circles lower and lower
while the sludge moils and crests.

Now we are about to lose our voices
we remember that tomorrow is our echo.
O the old songs, the good days:
bad faith and civil disobedience,
sloppy scholarship and tooth decay.
Now the age of footnotes is ours.
Ibid, ibid, ibid, ibid, ibid.

While the rivers thickened and fish
rose like vomit, the students of water
stamped each fish with its death date.
Don't let a chance like this go by,
they thought, though it went by
as everything went by — towers
of water flecked by a confetti
of topsoil, clucked tongues, smug
prayers. What we paid too much for
and too little attention to,
our very lives, all jumbled
now and far too big in aggregate
to understand or mourn, goes by,
and our all eloquence places its
weight on the spare word *goodbye*.

One-liners

THE NEEDLE'S EYE, THE LENS

Here comes the blind thread to sew it shut.

LUST ACTS

But desire is a kind of leisure

SLEEP

border with no country

HOW CAREFUL FIRE CAN BE

is not for fire to tell

Spiritual Life

To be warm, build an igloo

No True Rhyme in English for "Silver"

"Pilfer" is true enough for me

DAWN

Insomnia, old tree, when will you shed me?

WHY I DIDN'T NOTICE IT

The moss on the milk is white

Premature Ejaculation

I'm sorry this poem's already finished

The Past

Grief comes to eat without a mouth

Snow

The dead are dreaming of breathing

from

Rising and Falling

(1979)

SPRING SNOW

Here comes the powdered milk I drank
as a child, and the money it saved.
Here come the papers I delivered,
the spotted dog in heat that followed me home

and the dogs that followed her.
Here comes a load of white laundry
from basketball practice, and sheets
with their watermarks of semen.

And here comes snow, a language
in which no word is ever repeated,
love is impossible, and remorse. . . .
Yet childhood doesn't end,

but accumulates, each memory
knit to the next, and the fields
become one field. If to die is to lose
all detail, then death is not

so distinguished, but a profusion
of detail, a last gossip, character
passed wholly into fate and fate
in flecks, like dust, like flour, like snow.

At night the mountains look like huge
dim hens. In a few geological eras
new mountains may
shatter the earth's shell
and poke up like stone wings.
Each part must serve for a whole.
I bring my sons to the base
of the foothills and we go up.
From a scruff of ponderosa
pines we startle gaudy swerves
of magpies that settle in our rising
wake. Then there's a blooming
prickly pear. "Jesus, Dad, what's that?"
Willy asks. It's like a yellow tulip
grafted to a cactus: it's a beautiful
wound the cactus puts out
to bear fruit and be healed.
If I lived with my sons
all year I'd be less sentimental
about them. We go up
to the mesa top and look down
at our new hometown. The thin air
warps in the melting light
like the aura before a migraine.
The boys are tired. A tiny magpie
fluffs into a pine far below
and farther down in the valley
of child support and lights
people are opening drawers.
One of them finds a yellowing
patch of newsprint with a phone
number penciled on it
from Illinois, from before they moved, before
Nicky was born. Memory
is our root system.

"Verna," he says to himself
because his wife's in another room,
"whose number do you suppose this is?"

LIVING AMONG THE DEAD

> *There is another world,*
> *but it is in this one.*
>   Paul Éluard

First there were those who died
before I was born.
It was as if they had just left
and their shadows would
slip out after them
under the door so recently closed
the air in its path was still
swirling to rest.
Some of the furniture came from them,
I was told, and one day
I opened two chests
of drawers to learn what the dead kept.

But it was when I learned to read
that I began always
to live among the dead.
I remember Rapunzel,
the improved animals
in the *Just-So Stories*, and a flock
of birds that saved themselves
from a hunter by flying in place
in the shape of a tree,
their wings imitating the whisk
of wind in the leaves.

My sons and I are like some wine
the dead have already bottled.
They wish us well, but there is nothing
they can do for us.
Sebastian cries in his sleep,
I bring him into my bed,
talk to him, rub his back.
To help his sons live easily
among the dead is a father's great work.
Now Sebastian drifts, soon he'll sleep.
We can almost hear the dead
breathing. They sound like water
under a ship at sea.

To love the dead is easy.
They are final, perfect.
But to love a child
is sometimes to fail at love
while the dead look on
with their abstract sorrow.

To love a child is to turn
away from the patient dead.
It is to sleep carefully
in case he cries.

Later, when my sons are grown
among their own dead, I can
dive easily into sleep and loll
among the coral of my dreams
growing on themselves
until at the end
I almost never dream of anyone,
except my sons,
who is still alive.

LEFT HAND CANYON

for Richard Hugo

The Rev. Royal Filkin preaches
tomorrow on why we are sad.
Brethren, Montana's a landscape
requiring faith: the visible
government arrives in trucks,
if you live out far enough.
If you live in town, the government's
gone, on errands, in trucks.

Let citizens go to meetings,
I'll stay home. I hate a parade.
By the time you get the trout
up through the tiny triangular
holes in the Coors cans, they're so
small you have to throw them back.
Glum miles we go
to Grandmother's house.

The earth out here doesn't bear us
up so much as it keeps us out,
an old trick of the beautiful.
Remember what Chief Left Hand said?
Never mind. Everything else
was taken from him,
let's leave his grief alone.
My Eastern friends ask me

how I like it in the West,
or God's country, as it's sometimes
called, though God, like a slumlord,
lives in the suburbs: Heaven.
And I don't live "in the West";

I live in this canyon among a few
other houses and abandoned
mines, vaccinations that didn't take.

IN MEMORY OF THE UTAH STARS

Each of them must have terrified
his parents by being so big, obsessive
and exact so young, already gone
and leaving, like a big tipper,
that huge changeling's body in his place.
The prince of bone spurs and bad knees.

The year I first saw them play
Malone was a high school freshman,
already too big for any bed,
14, a natural resource.
You have to learn not to
apologize, a form of vanity.
You flare up in the lane, exotic
anywhere else. You roll the ball
off fingers twice as long as your
girlfriend's. Great touch for a big man,
says some jerk. Now they're defunct
and Moses Malone, boy wonder at 19,
rises at 20 from the St. Louis bench,
his pet of a body grown sullen
as fast as it grew up.

Something in you remembers every
time the ball left your fingertips
wrong and nothing the ball
can do in the air will change that.
You watch it set, stupid moon,
the way you watch yourself
in a recurring dream.

You never lose your touch
or forget how taxed bodies
go at the same pace they owe,
how brutally well the universe
works to be beautiful,
how we metabolize loss
as fast as we have to.

WAKING AT DUSK FROM A NAP

In the years that pass through
an afternoon's dream, like tape
at Fast Forward, there are
syllables, somehow, in the waterfall,
and in the dream I hear them each
clearly, a classroom
of children reciting their names.
I am not in the dream; it's as if I am
the dream, in which such distinctions
go without saying. And in which
a confusion I may soon have — did I
wake at dawn or dusk? — seems
anticipated: a strand of stars
goes by, like elephants spliced
trunk-to-tail in children's books
or ivory carvings, and the dream won't say
if they're through for the night
or amiably headed for work.

And the dream — and once, I remember,
it seemed I was the dream —
the dream tilts up to pour me out.

For an instant when I wake
there's a whir, perhaps of props
and stagehands, and a laggard star

scrambles over the transom.
The grainy world with its sworls
and lesions, its puckering dusk light,
its dimming patina, its used and casual
beauty, reassembles itself exactly.
And I climb down from bed, gather
my spilled book from the floor,
and watch the lights come on
in the valley, like bright type
being set in another language.

Eyes:

the only parts of the body the same
size at birth as they'll always be.
"That's why all babies are beautiful,"
Thurber used to say as he grew
blind — not dark, he'd go on
to explain, but floating in a pale
light always, a kind of candlelit
murk from a sourceless light.
He needed dark to see:
for a while he drew on black
paper with white pastel chalk
but it grew worse. Light bored
into his eyes but where did it go?
Into a sea of phosphenes,
along the wet fuse of some dead
nerve, it hid everywhere and couldn't
be found. I've used up
three guesses, all of them
right. It's like scuba diving, going down
into the black cone-tip that dives
farther than I can, though I dive
closer all the time.

Bud Powell, Paris, 1959

I'd never seen pain so bland.
Smack, though I didn't call it smack
in 1959, had eaten his technique.
His white-water right hand clattered
missing runs nobody else would think
to try, nor think to be outsmarted
by. Nobody played as well
as Powell, and neither did he,
stalled on his bench between sets,
stolid and vague, my hero,
his mocha skin souring gray.
Two bucks for a Scotch in this dump,
I thought, and I bought me
another. I was young and pain
rose to my ceiling, like warmth,
like a story that makes us come true
in the present. Each day's
melodrama in Powell's cells
bored and lulled him. Pain loves pain
and calls it company, and it is.

Foul Shots: A Clinic

for Paul Levitt

Be perpendicular to the basket,
toes avid for the line.

Already this description
is perilously abstract: the ball
and basket are round, the nailhead
centered in the centerplank
of the foulcircle is round,
and though the rumpled body

isn't round, it isn't
perpendicular. You have to draw
"an imaginary line," as the breezy

coaches say, "through your shoulders."
Here's how to cheat: remember
your collarbone. Now the instructions
grow spiritual — deep breathing,
relax and concentrate both; aim
for the front of the rim but miss it
deliberately so the ball goes in.
Ignore this part of the clinic

and shoot 200 foul shots
every day. Teach yourself not to be
bored by any boring one of them.

You have to love to do this, and chances
are you don't; you'd love to be good
at it but not by a love that drives
you to shoot 200 foul shots
every day, and the lovingly unlaunched
foul shots we're talking about now —
the clinic having served to bring us
together — circle eccentrically
in a sky of stolid orbits
as unlike as you and I are
from the arcs those foul shots
leave behind when they go in.

In Memory of W. H. Auden

1.
His heart made a last fist.
The language has used him
well and passed him through.

We get what he collected.
The magpie shines, burns
in the face of the polished stone.

2.

His was a mind alive by a pure greed
for reading, for the book
which "is a mirror,"
as Lichtenberg said: "if an ass
peers into it, you can't expect
an apostle to look out."

It was a mediating mind.
There were the crowds like fields of waving wheat
and there was the Rilkean fire
he didn't like
at the bottom of the night.
He loomed back and forth.
The space shrank.
The dogs of Europe wolved
about the house,
darks defining a campfire.

3.

My friend said Auden died
because his face
invaded his body.
Under the joke is a myth —
we invent our faces:
the best suffer most and it shows.
But what about the face
crumpled by a drunk's Buick?
Or Auden's
face in its fugue of photographs
so suddenly resolved?
It isn't suffering that eats us.

4.
They were not painting about suffering,
the Old Masters. Not the human heart but
Brueghel turns the plowman away
for compositional reasons
and smooths the waters for a ship he made
expensive and delicate.
The sun is implied by how
the sure hand makes the light fall
as long as we watch the painting.
The sure hand is cruel.

THE ICEHOUSE, POINTE AU BARIL, ONTARIO

Each vast block in its batter
of sawdust must have weighed
as much as I did. The sweat
we gathered running down
the path began to glaze.
We could see our breaths,
like comic strip balloons
but ragged, grey, opaque.

A warehouse of water on an island.
Once we arrived by seaplane:
the island looked like a green footprint.
Someone in a hurry saved time
by not sinking with each step.

In the icehouse I'd clear my name
on a block of ice and the dank film
of sawdust on my finger was as dense
as parts of grown-up conversation,
the rivalry of uncles and managing
money. The managers I knew
wore baseball caps and yelled.

As for money, I thought it was like food.
When blueberries were in season
we ate them all the time.

I always hoped to find a pickerel
in some block of ice
I was signing. Eyes frozen clear,
the tiny teeth like rasps on a file, the head
tapering to so fine a point it seemed
it could drill its way out. . . .
I'd smear the block clean with both hands cold
white under their gloves of sawdust.
Look here, I'd say clearly.

Long

for Stanley Plumly

It's about to be too late.
Every shred of the usual weather
is precious and sexual as it goes,
the way the links of a fugue become
one another's strict abandonments.

As for the future, it will not swerve.
Fire sleeps in the tree. Which tree?
Fire sleeps without dreaming and cannot
say. If we call the future's name
it becomes our name, by echo.

And from the dead, not even
a plea that we leave them
alone, each dead locked
in its dead name. If the dead complained,
they would say we summon them poorly,

dull music and thin wine, nor love
enough for the many we make,
much less for the melted dead
in their boxes. Above them
we talk big, since the place is vast

and bland if we tire of looking closely,
washed bland by light from what light
lets us see, our study,
the scripture of matter,
our long narcosis of parting.

Selected Translations,
Made with Mary Feeney,
from the
Prose Poems of Jean Follain

(1979)

ON EASTER SUNDAY the old man puts jewelry onto the wrists, ears, and neck of a long-haired woman. Already hitched to the black and yellow carriage, the glistening bay mare whinnies. A sailor sings by an engraving of the end of the world with Christ in the billowy heavens, the dead caught in their shrouds, leaving their graves. Time fills up with a future that may be fearsome. A child goes by on the road, wearing a motionless garter snake for a bracelet. How hot this long day beginning a century will be! Housebound, a deformed girl closes her blue eyes.

ONE DAY I suddenly notice this object within my sight for ten years and which in fact I had never truly seen. Likewise men forget the knick-knacks in their bedrooms, the patterns of their wallpaper, the faces on their andirons, until the day death takes them, as the saying goes, without formalities. Suddenly this forgotten bowl speaks to me, imposes its presence. I'm afraid it will fall from my hands, and on the rug depicting two elephants and their howdahs nothing will be left of it but shining fragments that have to be picked up sadly. The bowl was once washed by chattering maidservants surrounded by clouds and vapors, framed in glints of copper and tin. The world was new. In those days many men killed. Now everything plots without them against nothingness, even in the capitals where torture chambers have come back again. I think it over, the bowl in my hands. Whatever craftsman fashioned it perhaps kept a proud look about him, a modest glance, was perhaps alone in the world.

THE FINENESS OF THINGS gives the universe nobility. Behind each thing a password lies hidden. These fragile cups, these crystal glasses, how carefully they must be put in the cupboard! The maid gets up on a chair when they belong on the highest shelf. They link us to the world whose tarnished images blur together. In the same way a boy, seeing old straw beehives, thinks of the Gauls' huts in his *History of France*. Suppose the boy's mother happens to say to him, "You're heartless," and the sentence echoes deeper and deeper inside him. The world around him is veiled, sadness hangs heavily on roofs with weathervanes depicting a variety of things, even racehorses ridden by their jockeys. Sadness covers everything, even toys. It's sadness for the end of the world, for the last judgment. "No," the child answers, "I'm not a bad boy, because I cried when grandfather died." "Maybe so," the mother comes back, "but you aren't always good." That's like telling him he's good sometimes, anyway. So the universe clears up again, things regain their glitter, clouds are proud and graceful. Once more, decorations and everyday things sparkle. You hear the saw grinding into wood, food boiling, even if it's one of those monotonous long days that persist in having been, long after the memory of them is gone.

SHE STOPS short at something said to her, holding at arm's length the plate she'd just put on the table. Outside, the air's pure, it seems nothing should be a secret. When the children shout too loud, she says to them, "Listen, I can't hear a thing." The children play all sorts of games under the table; they're soldiers, generals, priests, then they become schoolteachers. Above them the table is being set. The dishes don't match anymore: one's all white, another has the branch of an indeterminate tree on it and on top of that a bird, pink as the branch. A third plate is hexagonal, one of its points chipped off. A fourth is rimmed in gold. Glasses have also been set. The forks are tin.

The knives have black handles. A little girl comes out of the next room, the one she wasn't supposed to go into. Walking along, she holds an outsized beginning geography book open in front of her and reads, stressing each syllable: "The earth is round like a ball." On the table now there are salt crystals and, on a large platter, the food in its sauce that looks like black lacquer.

THERE ARE MOMENTS the child isn't drawn to his toys, whether old or brand new. He feels the silence surrounding objects in the house, which keeps its special smell in spite of everything. Quite differently from toys the elements will attract him, above all fire and water. It's a turbid joy he'll feel watching a cardboard horse burn. Likewise he'll be able to change dry earth to mud he'll handle for hours, eager for mystery. There's also, for his delight, sumptuous matter: the soot from tall chimneys forms thick shells, forms crusts, and falls off in slabs. Didn't this soot, pulverized and mixed with wine, once serve as ink for village scriveners? As night comes on, the child's curiosity subsides. While sometimes a drunk, singing to keep his hopes up, pack slung over his shoulder, starts on his floundering but irreversible path into the silent traitor of a pond, where he dies.

THE WOMEN washing dishes were full of talk. You could hear glasses and bowls colliding. Through calm windows you could see a large shed containing several wheels, one from a tricycle, another from a child's stroller pushed so long, so ceremoniously beneath the sycamores. Sometimes the women would stop; still holding porcelain plates in their hands, they'd tilt their heads, squinting a little, trying to remember a forgotten name or date. At their feet, the cat licked milk from a saucer. The future was nonetheless full of hideous landscapes, bloody barracks bitten by the wind, stupor in armored railroad cars. For the time being, it was unheard of. There was the neatness of table settings and shining kitchen utensils touching the softened skin of the dish-washers, these women who, in a couple of hours, would say: "It's getting dark, let's light the lamps, you can't see a thing."

*F*LIES die on the sticky ribbon hung from the ceiling. The rings on the coal stove burners fit into each other perfectly. The walls were a problem: which color would show the dirt least? They decided on ochre. In the bedrooms, all kinds of wood, from oak to Brazilian rosewood. The whisk of brooms and feather dusters can't keep the noise out. If it's really nice weather, they open the windows wide. The hands on the clock never stop. If you leaned out a window you'd see silhouettes carrying a briefcase or a tool, sometimes followed by a dog. Children stay indoors, wrapped in warm, well-made clothes with every button tight. You think you see a faint tremor on the horizon.

*T*HERE ARE THOSE who would like to have all catastrophes happen and be done with — so long as they're sure that after-wards all will be calm for a long time, with the finest hint of the eternal in the air. And, at most, once in a while, the dust of tragedy will rise from a broken column, a theatrical column that wouldn't look quite right. In this life of keeping up the old appearances you'd need to put up a good-natured front. The insects would still be there, multiform and well armored; there'd be plenty of time to study them, a drink, if you wanted one, close at hand. The hand would be wearing starched cuffs, like those on finely drawn hands you still find pointing the way down some small town hall's yellowed corridors. So it would be a life of happy bit players: docile dogs, cunning cats, comely house-maids, bakers, delivery boys, chimney-sweeps, cobblers, punc-tilious jewelers. "But wouldn't a life like that be despicable, even with all the spectacular sunsets it might entail?" you think, called back to the restlessness of days present.

*I*N 1880, hair counts a lot in the impression women make; it can add to their attraction. In the morning, through a half-opened window, you see those long falls of hair — black, auburn, brown, red, or blond — that make the woman look like some enchanted animal. Their hair spills all the way below the waist, to the place God reads as easily as the heart, according to the preacher. Straight-haired women envy those with naturally curly hair. They talk of it as if it were a private income. "Oh what thick wavy hair she's got," they say. Raising his head from time to time to see the morning sky glint or darken, the gardener tends his beds. His rake rasps along with the noise a comb makes in tufts full of static, coming to again after the languid night. The hair is slowly arranged in front of a bevelled dresser mirror as the smell of lilacs floats through the window. It takes concentra-tion to get the hairpins right. There are days when strict buns refuse to be built up after you've unwoven the long braids made for those hours of sleep.

SCHOOLCHILDREN holding hands pose for a photographer from the postcard company. Just then a bell tolls a passing: suffering has had its way with a proud body. For nights on end a cramped room would be light, dark, then light again; a tattered book lay there on a table. While the children, near a grey statue, stare at the lens, one branch of a rosebush quakes; it will be blurred in the photograph, but the children will show up clearly in their bulky clothes. Their faces have a modest look, suspicious, already cruel, the town cynic might say.

PEOPLE try to fight time. A pet is a help. But the number of infinitesimal creatures populating a house — how could you ever count them? They occupy the grooves in the floor, the rafters; they settle from peak to foundations, even in the flour supply. If one of them walks on a windowpane, a slender index finger annihilates it: all of it goes under: respiratory and circulatory systems, sense organs. But it might, on the other hand, walking on the rim of a big heavy copper pot, drop into a thick brown sauce, die there like the worker who lost his step and fell into a vat of molten steel one starry night.

THE WOMEN say: "It looks like rain." The clouds burst, they all go inside and open the linen closet so they'll feel secure. Counting the sheets claims its due importance. On stormy days they'll comfort each other: "It won't hit us," one of them says, "there's the lightning rod at the school, and on the bank, and the cathedral. Oh, maybe if we lived a mile away, out in the open, but not here!" If a gale blows up while someone's visiting, they tell her as she leaves: "You can't be serious, you can't go home in this mess, it's impossible." So she stays, and her sweet face is livid that instant the sky lights up.

from

Flood

(1982)

NEW

The long path sap sludges up
through an iris, is it new
each spring? And what would
an iris care for novelty?
Urgent in tatters, it wants
to wrest what routine it can
from the ceaseless shifts
of weather, from the scrounge
it feeds on to grow beautiful
and bigger: last week the space
about to be rumpled
by iris petals was only air
through which a rabbit leapt,
a volley of heartbeats hardly
contained by fur, and then the clay-
colored spaniel in pursuit
and the effortless air
rejoining itself whole.

HOUSEWORK

How precise it seems, like a dollhouse,
and look: the tiniest socks ever knit
are crumpled on a chair in your bedroom.
And how still, like the air inside a church
or basketball. How you could have lived
your boyhood here is hard to know,

unless the blandishing lilacs
and slant rain stippling the lamplight
sustained you, and the friendship of dogs,
and the secrecy that flourishes in vacant lots.
For who would sleep, like a cat in a drawer,
in this house memory is always dusting,

unless it be you? I'd hear you on the stairs,
an avalanche of sneakers, and then the sift
of your absence and then I'd begin to rub
the house like a lantern until you came back
and grew up to be me, wondering how to sleep
in this lie of memory unless it be made clean.

BYSTANDERS

When it snowed hard, cars failed
at the hairpin turn above the house.
They'd slur off line and drift
to a ditch — or creep back down,
the driver squinting out from a half-
open door, his hindsight glazed
by snow on the rear window
and cold breath on the mirrors.
Soon he'd be at the house to use
the phone and peer a few feet out
the kitchen window at the black
night and insulating snow.
Those were the uphill cars. One night
a clump of them had gathered
at the turn and I'd gone out
to make my usual remark —
something smug about pride disguised
as something about machines and snow —
and to be in a clump myself. Then
over the hillbrow one mile up the road

came two pale headlights and the whine
of a car doing fifty downhill through
four tufted inches of snow atop a thin
sheet of new ice. That shut us up,
and we turned in thrall, like grass
in wind, to watch the car and all
its people die. Their only chance
would be never to brake, but to let
the force of their folly carry them, as if
it were a law of physics, where it would,
and since the hill was straight until
the hairpin turn, they might make it
that far, and so we unclumped fast
from the turn and its scatter of abandoned cars;
and down the hill it came, the accident.
How beautifully shaped it was, like an arrow,
this violent privation and story
I would have, and it was only beginning.
It must have been going seventy when it
somehow insinuated through the cars
we'd got as far away from as we could,
and it left the road where the road left
a straight downhill line. Halfway
down the Morgans' boulder- and stump-
strewn meadow it clanged and yawed,
one door flew open like a wing, and then
it rolled and tossed in the surf of its last
momentum, and there was no noise from it.
The many I'd imagined in the car were only one.
A woman wiped blood from his crushed
face with a Tampax, though he was dead,
and we stood in the field and stuttered.
Back at the turn two collies barked
at the snowplow with its blue light
turning mildly, at the wrecker, at the police
to whom we told our names and what we saw.
So we began to ravel from the stunned
calm single thing we had become

by not dying, and the county cleared
the turn and everyone went home, and, while
the plow dragged up the slick hill the staunch
clank of its chains, the county cleared the field.

TWINS

One may be a blameless bachelor,
and it is but a step to Congreve.
Marianne Moore

When I was eleven and they
were twenty-two, I fell in love
with twins: that's how I thought
of them, in sum, five run-on
syllables, Connie-and-Bonnie.
They were so resolutely given
as a pair — like father-and-
mother — I never thought to prefer one,
warm in her matching bed
like half an English muffin
in a toaster, though Bonnie
was blonde, lithe, walleyed,
angular, and fey. And Connie
was brunette, shiny-eyed, and
shy, as most true flirts
describe themselves, over and over.

And shouldn't love be an exclusive
passion? To fall in love with twins
made me unfaithful in advance?
It made me paralyzed, or I made
it — my love doubled forever
into mathematical heaven — paralysis.
Frocks rhyme and names confuse
and the world is thicker with sad

futures than lost pasts. And I,
who hoarded names like marbles,
how could I say what I knew?
Indeed, how can I say it now?
I knew the two meanings of *cleave*.
I looked into those eyes I loved,
two brown, two blue, and shut my own
(grey) from any light but mine
and walked straight home and kissed
my parents equally and climbed my growing
body's staircase to the very tip of sleep.

GOOD COMPANY

At dinner we discuss marriage.
Three men, three women (one couple
among us), all six of us wary.
"I use it to frighten myself."
Our true subject is loneliness.
We've been divorced 1.5 times
per heart. "The trick the last half
of our lives is to get our work done."
The golfer we saw from the car
this afternoon, his angered
face in bloom with blood, lashed
his strict ball for going where he'd hit it.
We watched him turn from a worse shot
yet and give us a look like our own,
and on we dawdled through
the afternoon toward dinner,
here. Here means the married
couple's house, of course.
The rest of us use so much time
being alone we don't entertain much.
The wind loops and subsides.
"What a fine night to sleep!"

Upstairs a book falls off a shelf.
We'll be sitting here ages hence:
the scent of lawns, good company, Sancerre,
fitful breezes suddenly earnest.
"What sense does marriage make now?
Both people want jobs, the sad
pleasures of travel, and also
want homes. They don't want dark houses
or to live with cats. They have lives
waiting up for them at home.
Take me, I must read half-an-hour
of Horace before I can sleep."
The conversation luffs. The last
bottle of wine was probably too much
but God we're happy here.
"My husband stopped the papers
and flea-bathed the dog
before he left." One of us has a friend
whose analyst died in mid-session,
non-directive to the end.
Now we're drifting off to our nine lives
and more. Melodramatic wind,
bright moon, dishes to do, a last
little puddle of brandy or not,
and the cars amble home:
the door, the stairs, the sheets
aglow with reticence and moonlight,
and the bed full to its blank brim
with the violent poise of dreams.

FUNERAL HOMES

So this is what's become of the idea
of purgatory, these long drawers
like card catalogues, as if the after-
life were a neglected scholarship.

Here every clue is false.
Funerals don't happen "at home,"
though death does, since the body
is home. And the houses,

solid as banks but adamantly
residential, imply that we can
take it with us, the shimmer
of matter we inhabit for a while,

or at least can leave it for safe-
keeping with substantial folks
who don't go out much, drink
on their ample porch, or burn lights

late, though nobody sleeps in such houses,
unless the night watchman cheats.
Better he read the classics all night
and think what a dead language means.

FLOOD

for James Tate

1. THE WATERS

If you stare out over the waters
on a bright day when the wind is down
and the waters move only to groom
themselves, turning their beautiful faces
a little to guess how the light looks
on them this way, and that. . . .

If you hear them, contented as they seem
to be, and quiet, so that they seethe,
like a slow fire, and their long syllable
is not broken into music. . . .

And if you should carry them with you
like the memory of impossible errands
and not know what you carry, nor how,
so that you feel inelevably mute,
as if from birth, then you will be apt
for speech, for books, and you'll be glib

though it torment you, and you'll rise
to the sacraments of memory and lie down
unable to forget what you can't name,
and the wine in your glass will be ink.

2. FLOOD PEAK
Over the rising waters,
like the silver of breath
on a mirror, the shadow
of a cloud luffs by.
This is the way it looks —
beautiful — from far away.

Closer, everything stinks
of the speed it's being ruined,
exploded, rot with a fever.
Doubtless the graves are open
below us and the roads go
everywhere at once.

The water is herding us
upstairs because the house
is swelling like a grain of rice.
We watch a bloated sow
float by, her teats like buttons
the water will undo from inside.

The window over the bed
doesn't rattle anymore,
its frame is so thick with sog.
We said we'd never sleep here
again and now there's nowhere else.

3. RECORD FLOOD
Rain pumped snakes from their holes
and rain was so much rain it began
to leak up and bear on its back

the froth of rain that came
to cover the rain that came before.
Rain with rain on its back goes

where its load needs to go,
all the way to brack, fatigue
from going, the surface always

falling into whatever it covers
until it is gone and the new land
looks as though it always looked

like this, no pod-like propane
tanks blooming against cliffs,
no road the old only know

where it was, no bodies waiting
for dental records, no big time.
Only the blue acres drenched by light.

4. TAKEN AT THE FLOOD
Suddenly the drizzle lifts
its dank voice: a slant
rain and then sleet
sizzles at the windows
like a fury so pure it's
dispersed by recognizing it,
one of those cramps you get
by loving your children wrongly
that only wrong love and all
your fatal habits will see
you through, though you
rant against them:
lordly as the froth

on the lip of the waterfall,
you urge them to carry you
over, and they do.

5. FLOOD LIGHT
Walking the prairies — sky so vast
and horizon so far around it seems
to fall away from you —

you sense the flood, drained
millennia ago. Here and there the earth
is cracked and scaled, reptilian.

And here and there, as the long light
pours down, you think how the rising
waters would bear up the prairie wind

and its ceaseless murmurs, how silent
this floor would be if the flood
should come again in water.

6. FLOOD PLAIN
You could pick one up, any one
from the scrupulous profusion
by which accident has sown them here,
smoother from their streambed tenure
than jagged from being strewn, and what

would you say you held? You could draw
one of them, or write the letters for *stone*
in some language, any one of them,
and what then could you say you held?
It would be a clear day, I would be with you,

and we would have a water-lathed box
full of the true history of itself,
to which the history of any treaty

is but a heart-broken footnote.
Only water can read such a book,
or write one. Think how long we've
agreed to love each other, and forgot
to care for that dwindling future, as if
we had the time the stones have, or the time
water takes to redistribute the stones.

7. EVERYWHERE
By the way its every
event is local and exact,
and by the reluctance of water
to rise and the way it climbs
its reluctance, so shall you know
flood, and by the way it compiles

the erasure of its parts
and takes to itself the local
until all but sky is water.
On this huge page no breath
will write. The text is already
there, restless, revising itself.

BURGLARY

for Dave Smith

The family will hate most
the way privacy itself
seems to have been stolen,
and ease and deepest sleep.
What *is* that noise? An owl
threshing the mouse-fluff
from its talons, a spot of blood
like a castemark above its beak.
A dog loping aslant across

the yard. Something that slurs
in the wall. Membranes,
the locked windows pass things
through both ways. The neighbors
sleep less well, and one shuns
her cellar for a week, with its smell
like a packet of ripped-open yeast
and its spoils a family wanted
to own and nobody wants to steal.
Another neighbor sits down to write,
needing to know the name
of something he can't say
without a name, the way
when we first wake we look
a little blurred and shapeless,
and by shaking off those waters
become unique and familiar
to ourselves again, inhabitants
of our names. The man writing
stops for a minute. He doesn't
yet have the name, but a better
reason to need it. He continues
to write. That's why writers
call it "working." From above
the neighborhood looks brighter tonight
than usual. Some of these lights,
as burglars would know, burn
to fool burglars. A light burns
where a man is writing.
One cellar light's been on
for a week by now, though we
can't see it from up here nor know
how we know it's burning.

PISSING OFF THE BACK OF THE BOAT
INTO THE NIVERNAIS CANAL

It's so cold my cock is furled
like a nutmeat and cold,
for all its warm aspirations
and traffic of urine. 37
years old and it takes me a second
to find it, the poor pink slug,
so far from the brash volunteer
of the boudoir. I arc a few
finishing stutters into the water.
Already they're converted,
opaque and chill. How com-
modious the dark universe is,
and companionable the stars.
How drunk I am. I shake
my shriveled nozzle and three
drops lurk out like syllables
from before there were languages. Snug
in my pants it will leak a whole sentence
in Latin. How like a lock-keeper's
life a penis biography would be,
bucolic and dull. What the penis
knows of sex is only arithmetic.
The tongue can kiss and tell.
But the imagination has,
as usual, most of the fun.
It makes discriminations,
bad jokes. It knows itself
to be tragic and thereby silly.
And it can tell a dull story well,
drop by reluctant drop.
What it can't do is be a body
nor survive time's acid work
on the body it enlivens,
I think as I try not to pitch
my wine-dulled body and wary

imagination with it into the inky
canal by the small force
of tugging my zipper up.
How much damage to themselves
the body and imagination
can absorb, I think as I drizzle
to sleep, and how much
the imagination makes
of its body of work
a place to recover itself.

SCHOOL FIGURES

for Susan

It's best to work before dawn:
fresh ice, its surface silvered
and opaque, and you scritch out
onto the milky ice, not avid
for grammar, too sleepy for speech.
It's not that you're marking time;
you're melting it grainy under
your runners. Each time you sweep

in your half-sleep around the figure
eight, your blades are duller
and record how far you've slid
from your margin of error, zero.
That's why you skate it backwards.
It's where you've been you have to go
again, alert enough to numb
every muscle memory but one.

So much learning is forgetting
the many mistakes for the few
lines clear of the flourishes

you thought were style, but were
only personality, indelible as
it seemed. Who but you could
forge those stern exclusions? Where
the line of concentration crosses

itself, cutting and tying its knot
both, there learning and forgetting
are one attention, and are the thrall
that pulls you stiff-ankled over
the ice before dawn, turning
over your shoulder as if you could
skate back into your first
path and get it right for once.

THE PENALTY FOR BIGAMY IS TWO WIVES

I don't understand how Janis Joplin did it, how she made her
voice break out like that in hives of feeling. I have a friend who
writes poems who says he really wants to be a rock star — the
high-heeled boots, the hand-held mike, the glare of underpants
in the front row, the whole package. He says he likes the way
music throws you back into your body, like organic food or
heroin. But when he sings it is sleek and abstract except for the
pain, like the silhouette of a dog baying at the moon, almost
liver-shaped, a bell hung from a rope of its own pure yearning.
Naturally his life is exciting, but sometimes I think he can't tell
the difference between salvation and death. When I listen to my
Janis Joplin records I think of him. Once I got drunk & sloppy
and told him I feared artists always had more fun and more
death, too, and how I had these strong feelings but nothing to do
with them and he said *Don't worry I'd trade my onion collection for a*
good cry, wouldn't you? I didn't really understand but poetry is
how you feel so I lie back and listen to Janis's dead voice run up
and down my body like a fire that has learned to live on itself

and I think *Here it comes, Grief's beautiful blow job.* I think about the painter who was said to paint with his penis and I imagine one of his portraits letting down a local rain of hair around his penis now too stiff to paint with, as if her diligent silence meant to say *You loved me enough to make me, when will I see you next?* Janis, I don't care what anybody thinks or writes, I don't care if my friend who writes poems is a beautiful fake, like a planetarium ceiling, I want to hold my life in my arms as easily as my body will hold forever the silence for which the mouth slowly opens.

NABOKOV'S DEATH

The solid shimmer of his prose
made English lucky that he wrote

plain English butterflies
and guns could read,

if they were fervent readers.
He loved desire. *Ada* could be

pronounced *Ah, Da!* — one
of those interlingual puns

he left, like goofy love notes,
throughout the startled house.

And yet we'll hold to our grief,
stern against grace, because we love

a broken heart, "the little madman
in his padded cell," as Nabokov

once described a fetus. For grief
is a species of prestige, if we mourn

the great, and a kind of power,
as if we had invented what we love

because it completes us. But
our love isn't acid: things deliquesce

on their own. How well he knew that,
who loved the art that reveals art

and all its shabby magic. The duelists
crumple their papier-mâché pistols.

The stage dead rise from the dead.
The world of loss is replete.

On the Porch at the Frost Place, Franconia, NH

for Stanley Plumly

So here the great man stood,
fermenting malice and poems
we have to be nearly as fierce
against ourselves as he
not to misread by their disguises.
Blue in dawn haze, the tamarack
across the road is new since Frost
and thirty feet tall already.
No doubt he liked to scorch off
morning fog by simply staring through it
long enough so that what he saw
grew visible. "Watching the dragon
come out of the Notch," his children
used to call it. And no wonder
he chose a climate whose winter
and house whose isolation could be

stern enough to his wrath and pity
as to make them seem survival skills
he'd learned on the job, farming
fifty acres of pasture and woods.
For cash crops he had sweat and doubt
and moralizing rage, those staples
of the barter system. And these swift
and aching summers, like the blackberries
I've been poaching down the road
from the house where no one's home —
acid at first and each little globe
of the berry too taut and distinct
from the others, then they swell to hold
the riot of their juices and briefly
the fat berries are perfected to my taste,
and then they begin to leak and blob
and under their crescendo of sugar
I can taste how they make it through winter. . . .
By the time I'm back from a last,
six-berry raid, it's almost dusk,
and more and more mosquitoes
will race around my ear their tiny engines,
the speedboats of the insect world.
I won't be longer on the porch
than it takes to look out once
and see what I've taught myself
in two months here to discern:
night restoring its opacities,
though for an instant as intense
and evanescent as waking from a dream
of eating blackberries and almost
being able to remember it, I think
I see the parts — haze, dusk, light
broken into grains, fatigue,
the mineral dark of the White Mountains,
the wavering shadows steadying themselves —
separate, then joined, then seamless:
the way, in fact, Frost's great poems,

like all great poems, conceal
what they merely know, to be
predicaments. However long
it took to watch what I thought
I saw, it was dark when I was done,
everywhere and on the porch,
and since nothing stopped
my sight, I let it go.

from

A Happy Childhood

(1985)

GOOD

I'd seen wallpaper — I had buckaroos all over my
bedroom — but my friend the only child had ceiling paper;
in the dark he had a flat sky, if stars make

a sky. Six feet above his bed, where the soul hovers
when the body's in doubt, he had a phosphorous
future, a lifetime of good marks for being alone.

He's an only child, you know, my parents would say.

OK, but I slept with no lid, like a shoe left out-
doors or an imaginary friend, with no sky to hold
him down nor light by which to watch him drift away.

Listen, my little mongoose, I know
the difference between this and love,
for I've had love, and had it taken away.

This feeling-sorry-for-ourselves-but-outward
is one of desire's shiftier shapes:
see how the deep of night is crept upon our love-

making, and how we believe what we disbelieve,
and find in our hopeful arms what we'd thought
to have thrown away, my stolen good,

the map by which we'll part, and love others.

.   .   .

Romantic, you could call him,

since he walks the balance beam
of his obsession like a triumphant
drunk passing a police test;

though, like a man in love
with a woman fools would find plain,
he doesn't turn aside for beauty;

he's a classicist, and studies
nightly a book so persistently good
he can't exhaust it, nor can it him.

Most of the time nothing happens here, we're fond
of saying. I love those stories and poems

an editor for *Scrotum* or *Terrorist Quarterly*
would describe that way, and besides,
every time in all my life I've said or heard

the phrase it's been a good lie, meaning
at least that crime and melodrama rates

are low enough that we can see, if we want,
the huge slow wheel of daily life, love and boredom,
turning deep in the ship-eating waters.

"The whole city of London uses the words *rich*
and *good* as equivalent terms," wrote Wesley
(1788), who failed to include in his whole city
the "honest poor," condemned by such a name
to improve their diet at the cost of honor.

"My good man" means "good for his debts,"
and not for nothing. What better faith

is there for the future than the braid of debt
we make, all of us? The day of reckoning
had better take its time: we're good for it.

I shouldn't pick on myself, but I do:
pimples and scabs and wens, warts, pustules,
the duff of the body sifting out, the dust

and sawdust of the spirit, blotches and slurs

and liver spots, the scar from the dogbite,
the plum-colored birthmark. . . . All this scuff
and tarnish and waste, these shavings

and leavings. . . . Deep in my body the future
is intact, in smolder, in the very bone,
and I dig for it like a dog, good dog.

After a week of sullen heat, the drenched air
bunched as if it needed to sneeze but couldn't,
the sky gives up its grip on itself and — good —

rain swabs the thick air sweet. The body's dirty
windows are flung open, and the spirit squints

out frankly. A kind of wink runs through
the whole failing body, and the spirit begins,

under its breath at first, talking to itself.
Mumbles, snickers, declamations, and next
it's singing loudly into the glistening streets.

Hi Mom, as athletes say on TV,
and here's a grateful hello to my mild

and courageous father. While I'm at it
I'd like to thank my teachers (though

not some — they know who they are) and
my friends, who by loving me freed

my poems from seeking love. Instead
they go their own strange ways

to peculiar moments like this one, when
the heart's good manners are their guide.

THE INTERPRETATION OF DREAMS

What animals dream of I do not know.
The urchin cat we rented with the house
was sun-stunned one minute and twitched

the next, pursued by humans, maybe.
The valley could be dreaming the haze
that filled it, both it and I

replete, like a wound
cat sleeping. The walled hilltowns
we drove to nights in search

of the perfect pasta also curled
in on themselves, like nutmeats.
How I loved those stone towns,

stark against fire, the houses
rising like tamed bluffs,
fortification as a way of life.

When I imagine an afternoon
nap in Gubbio, let's say, I dream
of light, mild cousin to fire,

bristling its blind rays
like a bottle-brush down house-
facades until they fleck the stony

streetbeds. Then I'd rise and walk
in diminishing circles *al centro,*
where there's a church and a square,

a blare of blank space amidst
all that habit and stricture.
How often I've arrived at myself

like that, as in a dream.
Nothing can be brought to an end
in the unconscious, where

the circuits of self-dramatization
complete themselves endlessly.
The dream-*work*, Freud called it,

"like fire*works* (my italics),
which require hours for their
preparation and then flare up

in a moment." Daydreams like mine
of Gubbio imitate such
condensation and release,

though they lack that umbilical
tether to the other world that makes
dreams art and daydreams gossip.

And daydreams can be broken
off at sluggish will, like mine,
but dreams have their own urgencies.

The other night I dreamed
I was shaking myself awake
beside that waif cat, dead now

for two years. "Let's go to Gubbio
tonight and eat tortellini."
How long it takes to make them right,

and how they flare up
in the mouth like sunspots,
both dense and evanescent.

SYMPATHETIC

In *Throne of Blood*, when they come to kill
Macbeth, the screen goes white. No sound.
It could be that the film has broken,
so some of us look back at the booth,

but it's fog on the screen, and from it,
first in one corner and then in another,
sprigs bristle. The killers close in further —
we're already fogged in by the story —

using pine boughs for camouflage,
and Birnam Forest comes to Dunsinane.
Even in Japanese, tragedy works:
he seems to extrude the arrows

that kill him — he's like a pincushion — ,
as if we grew our failures and topples,
as if there were no larger force than will,
as if his life seemed strange to us

until he gave it up, half-king, half-
porcupine. We understand. We too were fooled
by the fog and the pines, and didn't
recognize ourselves, until too late, as killers.

ON A DIET

> *Eat all you want*
> *but don't swallow it.*
> Archie Moore

The ruth of soups and balm of sauces
I renounce equally. What Rorschach saw
in ink I find in the buttery frizzle
in the sauté pan, and I leave it behind,
and the sweet peat-smoke tang of bananas,
and cream in clots, and chocolate. I give
away the satisfactions of food and take
desire for food: I'll be travelling light

to the heaven of revisions. Why be
adipose: an expense, etc.,
in a waste, etc.? Something like
the body of the poet's work, with its
pale shadows, begins to pare and replace
the poet's body, and isn't it time?

WHIPLASH

That month he was broke,
so when the brakes to his car
went sloshy, he let them go.
Next month his mother came
to visit, and out they went
to gawk, to shop, to have something

to do while they talked besides
sitting down like a seminar
to talk. One day soon he'd fix
the brakes, or — as he joked
after nearly bashing a cab
and skidding widdershins
through the intersection
of Viewcrest and Edgecliff —
they'd fix him, one of these
oncoming days. We like
to explain our lives to ourselves,
so many of our fictions
are about causality — chess
problems (where the *?!* after
White's 16th move marks
the beginning of disaster),
insurance policies, box scores,
psychotherapy ("Were your
needs being met in this
relationship?"), readers' guides
to pity and terror — , and about
the possibility that because
aging is relentless, logic too
runs straight and one way only.

By this hope to know how
our disasters almost shatter us,
it would make sense to say
the accident he drove into
the day after his mother left
began the month he was broke.
Though why was he broke?
Because of decisions he'd made
the month before to balance
decisions the month before that,
and so on all the way back
to birth and beyond, for his
mother and father brought
to his life the luck of theirs.

And so when his car one slick day
oversped its dwindling ability
to stop itself and smacked two
parked cars and lightly kissed
another, like a satisfying
billiards shot, and all this action
(so slow in compression and
preparation) exploded so quickly,
it seemed not that his whole life
swam or skidded before him,
but that his whole life was behind
him, like a physical force,
the way a dinosaur's body
was behind its brain and the news
surged up and down its vast
and clumsy spine like an early
version of the blues; indeed,
indeed, what might he do
but sing, as if to remind himself
by the power of anthem that the body's
disparate and selfish provinces
are connected. And that's how
the police found him, full-throated,
dried blood on his white suit
as if he'd been caught in a rust-
storm, song running back and forth
along his hurt body like the action
of a wave, which is not water,
strictly speaking, but a force
that water welcomes and displays.

BAD

Dew, sweat, grass-prickle, tantrums,

lemonade. One minute summer is all balm
and the next it's boredom and fury,

the library closed, the back yard blandly

familiar. The horizonless summer
recedes with a whoosh on all sides

like air being sucked out of a house

by a tornado, and there in the dead
center stands a child with a crumpling

face, whom somebody soon will call bad.

Beloved of mothers, too good in school and manners
to be true, can this unctuous wimp be real?

He'd be less dangerous if he had no good
at all in him, this level teaspoonful of virtue,

this festoon of fellowship, most likely
to succeed by filling in the blanks and hollows

like a fog or flood. Every morning he counts
his blessings backwards: he's not a crook,

not a recent thief, hates only the despised, and
(here it comes up his throat like a flag) he's not bad.

To pay a bad debt with bad coin, to breathe
bad air between bites (bad bites, an ortho-
dontist would say) of bad food, or worse,
food gone bad. . . .
                    By such a token *bad*
means discreditable, that hope is a bad lien
on belief, as if there were no evil but mis-
judgment, bad budgeting,
                              or in the case

of those teeth, bad genes. But let's say it:
evil exists, because choice does, and because
luck does and the rage that is luck's wake.

Here's bad luck for you: on your way to buy
shoelaces you're struck by a would-be suicide
as you pass beneath the Smith Tower. He's saved
and you're maimed, and long after he's released
he comes to visit you in the hospital and you'd

rip his lungs out of his trunk with your poor bare
hands if they'd obey you anymore, though as luck
would have it, they won't. Or, after the operation
cleared out every one of his cancer cells, a new crop
of them blooms along the line of the incision.

All the wrapping paper stuffed into the fireplace
Christmas morning, and all the white and brown
bags, the wax and butcher's paper, the shimmers

and crinkles of spent foil, plastic wrap in shrivels,
the envelopes ripped open 2500 miles away.

And the letters unfolded which are neither true
nor false, bad nor better, but all that the hurt heart

would cook or eat, or give and take. The ghosts
that swirl and stall and dive in the wind
like daunted kites. That we are all old haunts.

The granular fog gives each streetlight
an aura of bright haze, like a rumor:
it blobs as far as it can from its impulse.

The way gossip is truest about who says it,
the world we see is about the way we see;

if this is truth, it's easier than we thought.
What's bad about such truth is needing
to have it, as if it were money or love,

each of which clings to those on whom
enough has long ago, luckily, been spent.

The year I had my impacted wisdom teeth
cracked and tweezered out, I took codeine

for pain and beyond, until a day I could feel
my body faking pain, for which I rewarded it
with codeine. In this exchange the bad

marriage of mind and body was writ large,
and that a good one is work which is work's pay,

and that blame is not an explanation of pain
but a prolonging of pain, and that marriage
isn't a sacrament, although memory is.

When Williams called the tufty, stubbled
ground around the contagious hospital

"the new world," did he mean monumental
Europe was diseased and America needs,
like a fire set against a fire, a home-

made virus? I think so. These may be
the dead, the sick, those gone into rage

and madness, gone bad, but they're our dead
and our sick, and we will slake their lips
with our very hearts if we must, and we must.

The Psychopathology
of Everyday Life

Just as we were amazed to learn
that the skin itself is an organ —
I'd thought it a flexible sack,
always exact — we're stunned
to think the skimpiest mental
event, even forgetting, has meaning.
If one thinks of the sky as scenery,
like photographs of food, one stills it
with that wish and appetite,
but the placid expanse that results
is an illusion. The air is restless
everywhere inside our atmosphere
but the higher and thinner it gets
the less it has to push around
(how else do we see air?) but itself.
It seems that the mind, too,
is like that sky, not shiftless;
and come to think of it, the body
is no slouch at constant commerce,
bicker and haggle, provide and deny.
When we tire of work we should think
how the mind and body relentlessly
work for our living, though since
their labors end in death we greet
their ceaseless fealty with mixed emotions.
Of course the mind must pay attention
to itself, vast sky in the small skull.
In this we like to think we are alone:
evolutionary pride: it's lonely

at the top, self-consciousness. We forget
that the trout isn't beautiful and stupid
but a system of urges that works
even when the trout's small brain is somewhere
else, watching its shadow on the streambed,
maybe, daydreaming of food.
Even when we think we're not,
we're paying attention to everything;
this may be the origin of prayer
(and if we listen to ourselves,
how much in our prayers is well-dressed
complaint, how much we are loneliest Sundays
though whatever we do, say, or forget
is prayer and daily bread):
Doesn't everything mean something?
O God who composed this dense
text, our only beloved planet
— at this point the supplicants look upward —
why have You larded it against our hope
with allusions to itself, and how
can it bear the weight of such
self-reference and such self-ignorance?

TARDY

There's so little of swift time, and what time
we have is so much like held breath, how could
I or anyone be late? Think how fast
the second half of life pays itself out,
faster the smaller it grows, like tape:
how, near the end, the fattened take-up reel
scarcely turns at all. Maybe you've stalled, too,
and dressed your vanity in bandages,
new clothes, and turned your bland back to and left
your mirror, in which you dwindled more the more
you strode away. Did you look back? Tiny

as you were then, how could you be on time,
short steps, short breath? Did you relax and lag?
I did. That's why I'm late. That's why I'm late.

LOYAL

They gave him an overdose
of anesthetic, and its fog
shut down his heart in seconds.
I tried to hold him, but he was
somewhere else. For so much of love
one of the principals is missing,
it's no wonder we confuse love
with longing. Oh I was thick
with both. I wanted my dog
to live forever and while I was
working on impossibilities
I wanted to live forever, too.
I wanted company and to be alone.
I wanted to know how they trash
a stiff ninety-five-pound dog
and I paid them to do it
and not tell me. What else?
I wanted a letter of apology
delivered by decrepit hand,
by someone shattered for each time
I'd had to eat pure pain. I wanted
to weep, not "like a baby,"
in gulps and breath-stretching
howls, but steadily, like an adult,
according to the fiction
that there is work to be done,
and almost inconsolably.

A Happy Childhood

Babies do not want to hear about
babies; they like to be told of giants
and castles.
Dr. Johnson

No one keeps a secret so well as a
child.
Victor Hugo

My mother stands at the screen door, laughing.
"Out out damn Spot," she commands our silly dog.
I wonder what this means. I rise into adult air

like a hollyhock, I'm so proud to be loved
like this. The air is tight to my nervous body.
I use new clothes and shoes the way the corn-studded

soil around here uses nitrogen, giddily.
Ohio, Ohio, Ohio. Often I sing
to myself all day like a fieldful of August

insects, just things I whisper, really,
a trance in sneakers. I'm learning
to read from my mother and soon I'll go to school.

I hate it when anyone dies or leaves and the air
goes slack around my body and I have to hug myself,
a cloud, an imaginary friend, the stream in the road-

side park. I love to be called for dinner.
Spot goes out and I go in and the lights
in the kitchen go on and the dark,

which also has a body like a cloud's,
leans lightly against the house. Tomorrow
I'll find the sweatstains it left, little grey smudges.

·   ·   ·

Here's a sky no higher than a streetlamp,
and a stack of morning papers cinched by wire.
It's 4:00 A.M. A stout dog, vaguely beagle,

minces over the dry, fresh-fallen snow;
and here's our sleep-sodden paperboy
with his pliers, his bike, his matronly dog,

his unclouding face set for paper route
like an alarm clock. Here's a memory
in the making, for this could be the morning

he doesn't come home and his parents
two hours later drive his route until
they find him asleep, propped against a streetlamp,

his papers all delivered and his dirty paper-
satchel slack, like an emptied lung,
and he blur-faced and iconic in the morning

air rinsing itself a paler and paler blue
through which a last few dandruff-flecks
of snow meander casually down.

The dog squeaks in out of the dark,
snuffling *me too me too*. And here he goes
home to memory, and to hot chocolate

on which no crinkled skin forms like infant ice,
and to the long and ordinary day,
school, two triumphs and one severe

humiliation on the playground, the past
already growing its scabs, the busride home,
dinner, and evening leading to sleep

like the slide that will spill him out, come June,
into the eye-reddening chlorine waters
of the municipal pool. Here he goes to bed.

Kiss. Kiss. Teeth. Prayers. Dark. Dark.
Here the dog lies down by his bed,
and sighs and farts. Will he always be

this skinny, chicken-bones?
He'll remember like a prayer
how his mother made breakfast for him

every morning before he trudged out
to snip the papers free. Just as
his mother will remember she felt

guilty never to wake up with him
to give him breakfast. It was Cream
of Wheat they always or never had together.

It turns out you are the story of your childhood
and you're under constant revision,
like a lonely folktale whose invisible folks

are all the selves you've been, lifelong,
shadows in fog, grey glimmers at dusk.
And each of these selves had a childhood

it traded for love and grudged to give away,
now lost irretrievably, in storage
like a set of dishes from which no food,

no Cream of Wheat, no rabbit in mustard
sauce, nor even a single raspberry,
can be eaten until the afterlife,

which is only childhood in its last
disguise, all radiance or all humiliation,
and so it is forfeit a final time.

In fact it was awful, you think, or why
should the piecework of grief be endless?
Only because death is, and likewise loss,

which is not awful, but only breathtaking.
There's no truth about your childhood,
though there's a story, yours to tend,

like a fire or garden. Make it a good one,
since you'll have to live it out, and all
its revisions, so long as you all shall live,

for they shall be gathered to your deathbed,
and they'll have known to what you and they
would come, and this one time they'll weep for you.

The map in the shopping center has an X
signed "you are here." A dream is like that.
In a dream you are never eighty, though

you may risk death by other means:
you're on a ledge and memory calls you
to jump, but a deft cop talks you in

to a small, bright room, and snickers.
And in a dream, you're everyone somewhat,
but not wholly. I think I know how that

works: for twenty-one years I had a father
and then I became a father, replacing him
but not really. Soon my sons will be fathers.

Surely, that's what middle-aged means,
being father and son to sons and father.
That a male has only one mother is another

story, told wherever men weep wholly.
Though nobody's replaced. In one dream
I'm leading a rope of children to safety,

through a snowy farm. The farmer comes out
and I have to throw snowballs well to him
so we may pass. Even dreaming, I know

he's my father, at ease in his catcher's
squat, and that the dream has revived
to us both an old unspoken fantasy:

we're a battery. I'm young, I'm brash,
I don't know how to pitch but I can
throw a lamb chop past a wolf. And he

can handle pitchers and control a game.
I look to him for a sign. I'd nod
for anything. The damn thing is hard to grip

without seams, and I don't rely only
on my live, young arm, but throw by all
the body I can get behind it, and it fluffs

toward him no faster than the snow
in the dream drifts down. Nothing
takes forever, but I know what the phrase

means. The children grow more cold
and hungry and cruel to each other
the longer the ball's in the air, and it begins

to melt. By the time it gets to him we'll be
our waking ages, and each of us is himself
alone, and we all join hands and go.

·   ·   ·

Toward dawn, rain explodes on the tin roof
like popcorn. The pale light is streaked by grey
and that green you see just under the surface

of water, a shimmer more than a color.
Time to dive back into sleep, as if into
happiness, that neglected discipline. . . .

In those sixth-grade book reports
you had to say if the book was optimistic
or not, and everyone looked at you

the same way: how would he turn out?
He rolls in his sleep like an otter.
Uncle Ed has a neck so fat it's funny,

and on the way to work he pries the cap
off a Pepsi. Damn rain didn't cool one weary
thing for long; it's gonna be a cooker.

The boy sleeps with a thin chain of sweat
on his upper lip, as if waking itself,
becoming explicit, were hard work.

Who knows if he's happy or not?
A child is all the tools a child has,
growing up, who makes what he can.

*Integration in, or adaptation to, a
human community appears as a
scarcely avoidable condition which
must be fulfilled before [our] aim of
happiness can be achieved. If it could
be done without that condition, it
would perhaps be preferable.*
　　　　　　　　　Freud

How much of the great poetry
of solitude in the woods is one
long cadenza on the sadness

of civilization, and how much
thought on beaches, between drowsing
and sleep, along the borders,

between one place and another,
as if such poise were home to us?
On the far side of these woods, stew,

gelatinous from cracked lamb shanks,
is being ladled into bowls, and
a family scuffs its chairs close

to an inherited table.
Maybe there's wine, maybe not. We don't
know because our thoughts are with

the great sad soul in the woods again.
We suppose that even now
some poignant speck of litter

borne by the river of psychic murmur
has been grafted by the brooding soul
to a beloved piece of music,

and that from the general plaint
a shape is about to be made, though
maybe not: we can't see into

the soul the way we can into
that cottage where now they're done with food
until next meal. Here's what I think:

the soul in the woods is not alone.
All he came there to leave behind
is in him, like a garrison

in a conquered city. When he goes
back to it, and goes gratefully
because it's nearly time for dinner,

he will be entering himself,
though when he faced the woods,
from the road, that's what he thought then, too.

MASTERFUL

They say you can't think and hit at the same time,
but they're wrong: you think with your body, and the whole

wave of impact surges patiently through you
into your wrists, into your bat, and meets the ball

as if this exact and violent tryst had been a fevered
secret for a week. The wrists "break," as the batting

coaches like to say, but what they do is give away
their power, spend themselves, and the ball benefits.

When Ted Williams took — we should say "gave" —
batting practice, he'd stand in and chant to himself

"My name is Ted Fucking Ballgame and I'm the best
fucking hitter in baseball," and he was, jubilantly

grim, lining them out pitch after pitch, crouching
and uncoiling from the sweet ferocity of excellence.

FAMILIAL

When the kitchen is lit by lilacs
and everyone's list is crumpled or forgot,
when love seems to work without plans

and to use, like an anthill, all its frenetic
extra energy, then we all hold,
like a mugful of cooling tea,

my grandmother's advice: *Don't ever
grow old.* But I'm disobedient
to the end, eager to have overcome

something, to be laved by this light,
to have gone to the heaven of grown-ups
even if my body cracks and sputters

and my young heart grows too thick.
I want my place in line, the way
each word in this genial chatter

has its place. That's why we call it
grammar school, where we learn to behave.
I understand why everyone wants

to go up to heaven, to rise,
like a ship through a curriculum
of locks, into the eternal light

of talk after dinner. What I don't
understand is why one would balk to die
if death were entry to such heaven.

RIGHT

We always talked about getting it right,
and finally, by making it smaller and smaller,
like inept diamond cutters, we did. We chiseled
love's radiant play and refraction

to a problem in tact and solved it
by an exact and mannerly contempt,

by the arrogance of severity,
by stubble, by silence, by grudge,
by mistaking sensibility for form,
by giving ourselves up to be right.

You have the right to be silent, blank
as an unminted coin, sullen or joyfully

fierce, how would we know? What's truly yours
you'll learn irremediably from prison.

You have the right to clamp your eyes shut,
not to assent nor to eat nor to use our only

toilet in your turn, but to hold your breath
and frail body like secrets, and to turn blue

and to be beautiful briefly to yourself.
And we have our rights, too, which you can guess.

. . .

There's fan belts stiffening out back for cars
they haven't made in fifteen years, but if one
of them geezer wagons wobbles in here, we got

the right fan belt for it. We got a regular
cat with a fight-crimped ear and a yawn pinker
than cotton candy in fluorescent light, and we

got the oldest rotating Shell sign on Route 17;
hell, we're a museum. You can get halfway
from here to days beyond recall, and the last

half you never had a chance at, from the start.

Too right, my son accuses me when I correct
his grammar, but then, like an anaconda
digesting a piglet and stunned by how much blood
he needs to get this one thing done, he pales,

and then he's gone, slipped totally inside
himself, someplace I can't get from here
or anywhere, and now I need to tease him out
from his torpid sulk, or to wait till he slithers

out on his own. Come to think of it, that's how
I got here, eager, willful, approximate.

Four months of his life a man spends shaving,
a third of it asleep or pacing his room in want
of the civil wilderness of sleep, like a zoo lion

surveying the domain of its metabolism,
and what slice of his life does he pass

mincing shallots, who loves cooking?
If time is money, it's inherited
wealth, a relic worn smooth and then

worn to nothing by pilgrims' kisses,
and there's no right way to keep or spend it.

Right as rain you are, rain that shrivels
the grapes and then plumps the raisins.
You were right when you felt peeled,
like a crab in moult, and right you were

when you chafed stiffly against your shell

and wanted out. You're condemned to be right,
to agonize with what's right as the future
invades you and to explain the inevitable
past as it leaves you to colonize yourself,

to be you, finally to stand up for your rights.

Gauche, sinister, but finally harmless because
flaky, somehow miswired, a southpaw

(there's no more a northpaw than there is a soft-
nosed realist: the curse and blazon of rectitude
is that even the jokes about you are dull,

and your fire is embers and cozy, grey at the edge
and pink in the middle, like a well-cooked steak),

a figure of fun, as someone outnumbered so often
is, and all because you bring me, and you're right,
my irresistible self, hand, outstretched, in the mirror.

On the way to the rink one fog- and sleep-thick
morning we got the word *fuck* spat at us,

my sister fluffed for figure skating and I in pads
for hockey. The slash of casual violence in it

befuddled me, and when I asked my parents
I got a long, strained lecture on married love.

Have I remembered this right? The past is lost
to memory. Under the Zamboni's slathering tongue
the ice is opaque and thick. Family life is easy.
You just push off into heartbreak and go on your nerve.

The Theme of the Three Caskets

> *Men and women are two locked caskets,*
> *each of which contains the key to the other.*
> Isak Dinesen

One gold, one silver, one lead: who thinks
this test easy has already flunked.

Or, you have three daughters, two humming-
birds and the youngest, Cordelia, a grackle.

And here's Cinderella, the ash-princess.
Three guesses, three wishes, three strikes and

you're out. You've been practicing for this
for years, jumping rope, counting out,

learning to waltz, games and puzzles,
tests and chores. And work, in which strain

and ease fill and drain the body like air
having its way with the lungs. And now?

Your palms are mossy with sweat.
The more you think the less you understand.

It's your only life you must choose, daily.

Freud, father of psychoanalysis,
the study of self-deception and survival,
saw the wish-fulfillment in this theme:

that we can choose death and make what we can't
refuse a trophy to self-knowledge, grey,
malleable, dense with low tensile strength

and poisonous in every compound.
And that a vote for death elects love.
If death is the mother of love (Freud wrote

more, and more lovingly, on mothers
than on fathers), she is also the mother
of envy and gossip and spite, and she

loves her children equally. It isn't mom
who folds us finally in her arms,
and it is we who are elected.

Is love the reward, or the test itself?

That kind of thought speeds our swift lives
along. The August air is stale in

the slack leaves, and a new moon thin
as a fingernail-paring tilts orange

and low in the rusty sky, and the city
is thick with trysts and spats,

and the banked blue fires of TV sets,
and the anger and depression that bead

on the body like an acid dew when it's hot.
Tonight it seems that love is what's

missing, the better half. But think
with your body: not to be dead is to be

sexual, vivid, tender and harsh, a riot
of mixed feelings, and able to choose.

THE HUMMER

First he drew a strike zone
on the toolshed door, and then
he battered against it all summer
a balding tennis ball, wetted
in a puddle he tended under
an outdoor faucet: that way
he could see, at first, exactly
where each pitch struck.
Late in the game the door
was solidly blotched and
calling the corners was fierce
enough moral work for any
man he might grow up to be.
His stark rules made it hard
to win, and made him finish
any game he started, no matter
if he'd lost it early.
Some days he pitched
six games, the last in dusk,
in tears, in rage, in the blue
blackening joy of obsession.
If he could have been also
the batter, he would have been,
trying to stay alive. Twenty-
seven deaths a game and all

of them his. For a real game
the time it takes is listed
in the box score, the obituary.
What he loved was mowing
them down. Thwap. Thwap.
Then one thwap low and outside.
And finally the hummer.
It made him grunt to throw it,
as if he'd tried to hold it
back, but it escaped. Thwap.

Wrong

There's some wrong that can't be salved,
something irreversible besides aging.

This salt, like a light in the wound it rankles. . . .
It seems the wound might exist to uncover
the salt, the anger, the petulance we hoard

cell by cell, treasure the body can bury.
As J. Paul Getty knew, the meek will

inherit the earth, but not the mineral rights.
And what's our love for the future but greed,
who can't let go the unbearable past?

By itself *wrong* spreads nearly five pages
in the *OED*, and meant in its ancestral forms
curved, bent, the rib of a ship — neither
straight, nor true, but apt for its work.

The heart's full cargo is so immense it's not

hard to feel the weight of the word
shift, and we might as well admit it's easy
to think of the spites and treacheries
and worse the poised word had to bear

lest some poor heart break unexplained, inept.

It's wrong to sleep late and wake like a fog,
and to start each paragraph of a letter with *I*,

and wrong to be cruel to others, the swarms
of others damp from their mutual exaltations,

and wrong to complain more than once
if others are cruel to you, wrong to be lonely,

to come home in spirals and not to unscrew
but to whistle and twist by yourself like a seed

which the wind will know how to carry
and the wind will know when to drop.

It's too quiet out there. There's something wrong.
I smell a rat. You can't fire me, I quit, the boss
will never pay enough, it's so hot in here I think

I'll take off my job. Then I ripped off her dress, then
I hit her, I was like a wild man, except I was ashamed.

I've read about creeps in the papers, they hear voices
and don't disobey. I don't obey one, not even me,

and I'm all of my voices. Creeps, I said, and Creeps,
I sang, but I'm one. So are you. Let me buy you a beer.
I'll bet you're full of good stories. Let me buy you another.

       •   •   •

Even in sleep, the world is smaller. In a dream
I want you to go somewhere with me, and you
won't come. When I wake there's fog at the waists

of the trees, like a sash. There are treetops
and treetrunks, and a smear where the two don't
join. It's wrong to be in this much pain. The bay
is out there somewhere. Yes. I can hear someone

singing badly over the waters. No. It's a radio
with a cracked speaker drilling through the fog,
faithfully towing a lobsterboat to its traps.

Maybe what's wrong, if *wrong* is the right word,
is that we like to think the body is defending us,
as if when some part of the world gets in you
that shouldn't, you're done for, and so

your antibodies run wild and do not stop
when the work they're designed for is done,

but they rage against the very body. What
little I know of the mind, I know it sometimes
works like that, if *works* is the right word,
and it is. Not the body, nor the mind, has a boss.

What's wrong is to live by correction, to be good
for a living — proofreader, inspector of public works — ,

to go into the tunnels of error like a rat terrier
and come out and know you will be fed for it.
Sop, mash, some dark velvety food rich as bogbottom,

some archival soup with one of every nutrient,
an unbearably dense Babel of foodstuffs, what you get

for knowing wrong when you see it, for knowing
what to do next and doing it well, for eating
the food and knowing there is nothing wrong with it.

Corms and bulbs into the ground, bone meal
buried with them like a pharaoh's retainers,
and an exact scatter of bark on top for mulch. . . .

And the rank weeds winter down there, too,
as if the mulch were strewn for them, as if
diligent worms broke ground for them; and who's

to say, turning this soil, that they're wrong?
The detection of wrong and the study of error
are lonely chores; though who is wrong by himself,

and who is by himself except in error?

Selected Translations from Martial

I, i

Here he is whom you read and clamor for,
tasteful reader, the very Martial world-
renowned for pithy books of epigrams
and not even dead yet. So seize your chance:
better to praise him when he can hear
than later, when he'll be literature.

VIII, lxxvi

"Tell me the truth, Mark," you insist,
"What do you really think?"
When you recite your poems or plead
a client's case, you cry,
"You can be candid with me, pal,
what do you really think?"
I won't refuse you now. I think
you're asking me to lie.

X, xxxi

You sold a slave just yesterday
for twelve hundred sesterces, Cal;
at last the lavish dinner you've
long dreamed about is in the pan.
Tonight! Fresh mullet, four full pounds!

You know I'll not complain, old pal,
about the food. But that's no fish
we'll eat tonight; that was a man.

V, xlv

You announce that you are beautiful
and insist that you are young;
Bassa, if either claim were true
you'd hold your blowsy tongue.

V, xviii

Because in December when the gifts fly —
napery, wax tapers, slim spoons, paper
and tall jars of dried damsons — I've sent you
only my home-brewed little books, don't think
me rude or stingy. I despise the gift-
giving system: the present as a lure
and the hook a request for a kickback,
the better the fly, the greedier the trout.
And so, Quintianus, when a poor man
sends his rich friend nothing, that's a gift.

X, xlix

Although you fill amethyst cups
with wine even more rare, you pour
for me a Sabine wine not three months
off the lees. Worse, this jejune dread
arrives in a gold cup. What for,
Cotta? The stuff is liquid lead.

VI, lxxxii

Someone we both know, Rufus, looked me
up and down the other day, as if I
were a novice gladiator. "Can you,"
he wryly wanted to know, "be the Martial
whose snide, metallic poems everyone knows
who's not deaf to a joke?" What could I say?
I smiled, I bowed, I did not lie. "Why then,"
he asked — his trap had sprung — , "your shockingly
bad cloak?" "It's all my verse has earned," I had
to tell him. Rufus, save us both from this
embarrassment: buy me a decent cloak.

VI, xxxvi

Papylus had a dong so long
and a nose so vast and subtle
that when it reared its ugly head
Papylus could smell trouble.

V, lvi

You wonder, Lupus, who's the best schoolmaster
for your son? To skirt certain disaster,
strike from your list all teachers of grammar
and rhetoric. Have him wholly ignore
anything by Cicero, and Virgil, too.
Read Tutilius? Tutilius who?
If the boy should scribble a few verses,
disinherit him. He could do far worse
than learn to make money — to play the harp

or tootle a flute. If he's not too sharp,
don't mope. It takes but paltry intellect
to be an auctioneer or architect.

III, lxi

"It's nothing," whatever
you beg for. If that's true,
it must be the very
nothing I'd deny you.

IX, xxi

Art and Cal have made a trade:
Art's land for Cal's young slave.
Who's the winner? Hard to guess:
they're both ploughing new furrows.

X, lxx

The long year I squeezed out a tiny book,
Potitus, so you chide me for torpor.
The wonder is that I could finish one,
the way my days blur each into the next.
By dawn I've left my calling card for friends
who don't respond, and sprayed with smarm and cheer
whomever I can reach. Me? I'm still dry.
Crosstown I trek to witness and seal
with my signet-ring a legal document
and then I'm off again, no time for lunch,
a blur and a good guy. Next one bigshot
or another, plus his minions, might stop

me for a chat, or some poor poet need
an audience. Someone needs a favor
and someone else wants to talk books.
By six my fellow Romans have worn me
to the nub, Potitus: a slack soak
in the baths and wan thanks for the dole.
What should I write, and when, after all this?

XII, lxix

The slave that Cinna's named his cook
is comeliest of a comely lot.
How good is he? Just have a look.
Oh what a palate Cinna's got.

X, xci

Surrounded by eunuchs and limp as a tissue,
Almo blames his Polla for bearing no issue.

XII, lvi

Ten times a year you're ill, Malingerus,
or more, then rise like Lazarus from bed.
It's we who are consumed, for we attack
each resurrection with a fierce volley
of gifts. Old friend, just once play dead for real.
But first, will us our investments back.

XI, xciii

Ted's studio burnt down, with all his poems.
Have the Muses hung their heads?
You bet, for it was criminal neglect
not also to have sautéed Ted.

VI, xii

That plush hair Fabulla wears?
It's hers, Fabulla swears.
I've no reason to deny it:
I saw Fabulla buy it.

V, x

Why is it modern poets are ignored
and only dead ones get adored?
That's how envy works, Regulus,
the dead make the safest rivals.
So we mourn Pompey's colonnade
and its nostalgic, leafy shade
just as our fathers praised the temple
Catulus restored not wisely nor too well.
Rome reads Ennius, though Virgil is to hand,
as Homer was a joke in his own land;
Menander's best plays were thought dull;
only Corinna knew her Ovid well.
So, little books, let's not rush to our fate.
Since death comes before glory, let's be late.

V, lxxxiii

You're hot to trot? Well then I'm not.
You've cooled? I'm ardent on the spot.
What's going on? Don't sulk, my pet:
I like you best as hard to get.

XII, xl

You lie and I concur. You "give"
a reading of your wretched verse
and I applaud. You sing and I
too lift my blowsy voice.

You drink, Pontificus, and I
drink up. You fart; I look away.
Produce a cribbage board; I'll find
a chance to lose, to pay.

There's but one thing you do without
me and my lips are sealed. Yet not
a minim of your money's trickled
down to me. So what?

You'll be good to me in your will?
No doubt you'd bounce a check from hell.
So don't hold back on my account;
if die you must, farewell.

V, xx

Old friend, suppose luck grants to us
days free of fret, that shadow life,
how would we live then? No foyers

to stall in, no butlers to schmooze,
no lawsuits, not one working lunch,
and no ancestral busts. Instead:
strolls, bars, bookshops, the fields,
shaded gardens, cold baths from the Aqua
Virgo and warm baths from the others —
these will be our office and our work.
We toil too much for others. Days
flicker by and then are billed,
one by one, to our accounts. Since we know
how, let's start really living now.

from

Foreseeable Futures

(1987)

HERD OF BUFFALO CROSSING THE MISSOURI ON ICE

If dragonflies can mate atop the surface tension
of water, surely these tons of bison can mince
across the river, their fur peeling in strips like old

wallpaper, their huge eyes adjusting to how far
they can see when there's no big or little bluestem,
no Indian grass nor prairie cord grass to plod through.

Maybe because it's bright in the blown snow
and swirling grit, their vast heads are lowered
to the gray ice: nothing to eat, little to smell.

They have their own currents. You could watch a herd
of running pronghorn swerve like a river rounding
a meander and see better what I mean. But

bison are a deeper, deliberate water, and there will
never be enough water for any West but the one
into which we watch these bison carefully disappear.

MEN IN DARK SUITS

Like talk overheard across water, they seem to have come
from far away louder and nearer than we thought, though
what we hear isn't what's said, but the blurred, rolling

surf of speech. They remind me of umpires trudging amiably
across the close-mown lawn — their burly ease, the way
the day seems not quite to have happened yet. The fervors

and dust, the long shadows, all these are still to come
and the men are drawing near. For all they seem at this
narrowing distance to be fathers roped together by banter,

won't we in our turn cross as familiarly the dwindling
field, ambling to low-voiced badinage about how like
them we've become, only to greet a cleric with a widow —

one of ours — crooked in his arm? But none
of this has happened yet. As steadily as afternoon
men come, joyless but content, across the ample grass.

Fellow Oddballs

The sodden sleep from which we open like umbrellas,
the way money keeps *us* in circulation, the scumbled lists
we make of what to do and what, God help us, to undo —

an oddball knows an oddball at forty or at 40,000
paces. Let's raise our dribble glasses. Here's to us,
morose at dances and giggly in committee,

and here's to us on whose ironic bodies new clothes
pucker that clung like shrink wrap to the manikins.
And here's to the threadbare charm of our self-pity.

For when the waiters, who are really actors between parts,
have crumbed for the last time our wobbly tables,
and we've patted our pockets for keys and cigarettes

enough until tomorrow, for the coat-check token
and for whatever's missing, well then, what next? God knows,
who counts us on God's shapely toes, one and one and one.

PHOTO OF THE AUTHOR WITH A FAVORITE PIG

Behind its snout like a huge button,
like an almost clean plate, the pig
looks candid compared to the author,

and why not? He has a way with words,
but the unspeakable pig, squat
and foursquare as a bathtub,

squints frankly. Nobody knows
the trouble it's seen, this rained-out
pork roast, this ham escaped into

its corpulent jokes, its body of work.
The author is skinny and looks serious:
what will he say next? The copious pig

has every appearance of knowing,
from his pert, coiled tail to the wispy tips
of his edible ears, but the pig isn't telling.

THE ACCOMPANIST

Don't play too much, don't play
too loud, don't play the melody.
You have to anticipate her
and to subdue yourself.
She used to give me her smoky
eye when I got boisterous,

so I learned to play on tip-
toe and to play the better half
of what I might. I don't like
to complain, though I notice
that I get around to it somehow.
We made a living and good music,
both, night after night, the blue
curlicues of smoke rubbing their
staling and wispy backs
against the ceilings, the flat
drinks and scarce taxis, the jazz life
we bitch about the way Army pals
complain about the food and then
re-up. Some people like to say
with smut in their voices how playing
the way we did at our best is partly
sexual. OK, I could tell them
a tale or two, and I've heard
the records Lester cut with Lady Day
and all that rap, and it's partly
sexual but it's mostly practice
and music. As for partly sexual,
I'll take wholly sexual any day,
but that's a duet and we're talking
accompaniment. Remember "Reckless
Blues"? Bessie Smith sings out "Daddy"
and Louis Armstrong plays back "Daddy"
as clear through his horn as if he'd
spoken it. But it's her daddy and her
story. When you play it you become
your part in it, one of her beautiful
troubles, and then, however much music
can do this, part of her consolation,
the way pain and joy eat off each other's
plates, but mostly you play to drunks,
to the night, to the way you judge
and pardon yourself, to all that goes
not unsung, but unrecorded.

Scenic View

From the scorch and poverty, from the cumin and opulence
of the Indian plains, dust gathers and spores convene.
Pollen, insects alive or in desiccate husk,

flecks of grit and commas lost in translation between
one of India's fifteen official languages and another —
all these are lofted by thermals toward the nival

heaven of the Himalayas, where it's so cold the warmth
of a dead insect — its last, grey-embered smidge
of decay — is enough to burn through the onionskin

snow crust an icy, open grave, which will soon
be pillaged by a phalangid spider who knows how
to snatch the remains without dislodging the rim

or becoming the depth, so delicate is the future
at 16,000 feet, where the genetic code burns like a pilot
light in every body, in each of the future's parasites.

Dog Life

Scuffed snout, infected ear, ticks like interest
on a loan. Butt of jokes that would, forgive me,
raise hair on a bald dog. Like the one about the baby

so ugly that to get a dog to play with it,
they had to tie a pork chop around the baby's neck.
Or, get this, when you're not working like a dog,

you're dogging it. Yet those staunch workers,
human feet, are casually called dogs, and they're
like miners or men who work in submarines,

hard men who call each other sons of bitches
when they're mad. No wonder it's not loyalty
to dogs that dogs are famous for, since it's men

who've made dogs famous. And don't we under-
stand about having masters, and having food?
Masters are almost good enough for us.

WRITER-IN-RESIDENCE

Blowsy geraniums, clay pots stained here
by water and blanched there by Rapid Gro,
a restive cat with the idle in its throat tuned high . . .

No wonder summer is like a series of paintings:
it lacks verbs, though *lacks* is a verb, and *is*.
Time sags like a slack flag. But Shop N Save

has sold summer's last raspberry, and beyond
the topspinning rim of the horizon, dutiful
fall is kneading a squall of work and metabolic

dither. If time is money, teachers are shabbiest
of all the summer rich. The rest of the year we rejoin
the poor we refused to use our educations to escape.

I'm a swarm of pleasantries for my first class.
O syllabus and charisma! But chill is in the air,
and the old rage for work gathers against my indolence.

MINUSCULE THINGS

There's a crack in this glass so fine we can't see it,
and in the blue eye of the candleflame's needle
there's a dark fleck, a speck of imperfection

that could contain, like a microchip, an epic
treatise on beauty, except it's in the eye of the beheld.
And at the base of our glass there's nothing

so big as a tiny puddle, but an ooze, a viscous
patina like liquefied tarnish. It's like a text
so short it consists only of the author's signature,

which has to stand, like the future, for what might
have been: a novel, let's say, thick with ambiguous life.
Its hero forgets his goal as he nears it, so that it's

like rain evaporating in the very sight of parched
Saharans on the desert floor. There, by chance, he meets
a thirsty and beautiful woman. What a small world!

HOPE

Beautiful floors and a lively
daughter were all he'd wanted, and then —
that the dear piñata of her head

not loose its bounty, the girl's
father scored the soles of her new shoes
with a pocketknife, that she not slide

nor skid nor turn finally upside-
down on the oak floors he'd sanded
and buffed slick long before she first

gurgled from her crib. Now he's dead
and she's eighty. That's how time
works: it's a tough nut to crack

and then a sapling, then a tree, and
then somebody else's floor long
after we ourselves are planted.

RECOVERY ROOM

How bright it would be, I'd been warned.
To my left an old woman keened steadily,
Help me, help me, and steadily a nurse delivered
false and stark balm to her crumpled ear:
You'll be all right. Freshly filleted, we lay

drug-docile on our rolling trays, each boat
becalmed in its slip. I was numb waist-down
to wherever I left off, somewhere between my waist
and Budapest, for I was pointed feet-first east.
I had the responsibility of legs, like tubes

of wet sand, but no sensation from them.
Anyone proud of his brain should try to drag
his body with it before bragging. I had to wait
for my legs and bowels and groin to burn
not with their usual restlessness but

back toward it from anesthetic null. I felt —
if *feel* is the right verb here — like a diver
serving time against the bends. And O
there were eight of us parked parallel
as piano keys against the west wall of that

light-shrill room, and by noon we were seven,
though it took me until I got to the surface
to miss her. Especially if half of me's been trans-
planted by Dr. Flowers, the anesthesiologist,
I'm divided, forgetful. I hated having an equator,

below which my numb bowels stalled and my bladder
dully brimmed. A terrible remedy for these
drug-triggered truancies was "introduced,"
as the night nurse nicely put it, and all
the amber night I seeped into a plastic pouch,

and by dawn, so eager was I to escape, and ever
the good student, I coaxed my bowels to turn
a paltry dowel. Here was proof for all of us:
my legs were mine to flee on once again.
Even a poet can't tell you how death enters

an ear, but an old woman whose grating voice
I hated and whose pain I feared died next to me
while I waited like a lizard for the first fizzles
of sensation from my lower, absent, better half:
and like a truculent champagne,

the bottom of my body loosed a few
petulant bubbles, then a few more,
and then. . . . You know the rest.
Soon they let me go home and I did.
Welcome back, somebody said. Back? Back?

BLACK BOX

Because the cockpit, like the snowy village in a paperweight,
parodies the undomed world outside, and because
even a randomly composed society like Air Florida

flight #7 needs minutes for its meeting, the tape
in the black box slithers and loops with its slow,
urinary hiss like the air-filtering system in a fall-

out shelter. What's normally on the tape? Office life
at 39,000 feet, radio sputter and blab, language
on automatic pilot. Suppose the flight should fail.

Cosseted against impact and armored against fire,
the black box records not time but history. Bad choice.
The most frequent last word on the black box

tape is "Mother." Will this change if we get
more female pilots? Who knows? But here's
the best exchange: "We're going down." "I know."

SCHOOLBOYS WITH DOG, WINTER

It's dark when they scuff off to school.
It's good to trample the thin panes of casual
ice along the track where twice a week

a freight that used to stop here lugs grain
and radiator hoses past us to a larger town.
It's good to cloud the paling mirror

of the dawn sky with your mouthwashed breath,
and to thrash and stamp against the way
you've been overdressed and pudged

into your down jacket like a pastel
sausage, and to be cruel to the cringing
dog and then to thump it and hug it and croon

to it nicknames. At last the pale sun rolls
over the horizon. And look!
The frosted windows of the schoolhouse gleam.

PUBERTY

Remember the way we bore our bodies to the pond
like raccoons with food to wash? Onto the blue,
smooth foil of the gift-wrapped water I slid

my embarrassing self. All the water I knew
was from books. I had read of the surfless Adriatic
and read how the North Atlantic erected by night

its wavering cliffs of fog and cul-de-sacs of ice,
only to turn to the dawn its chill, placid cheek.
But twitch and thrash in my chair as I might,

it was true what the swimming teacher told me:
once you learn how to float, it's almost impossible
to go under. I tried and tried, and so I can tell you

how we greet the news by which we survive: with rage.
A bucolic boy adrift on a Xenia, Ohio, pond?
Not on your life. Like you, I gulped and learned to swim.

BLUE NOTES

How often the blues begin early morning.
In the net of waking, on the mesh: bitter dew.
It's as if we'd been watered with nightmares

and these last squibs were the residue,
a few splatters from an evaporated eloquence
we can't reconstruct for all the cocaine

in Bogotá or winter wheat in Montana.
The blues tick in the wrist, even as the body
trudges its earnest portage to the shower.

Fight fire with fire and water with water.
You know that smirk in the blues? It turns out
the joke's on us. Each emotion lusts for its opposite —

which is to say, for itself. Our water music
every morning rains death's old sweet song,
but relentless joy infests the blues all day.

VASECTOMY

After the vas deferens is cut, the constantly
manufactured sperm cells die into the bloodstream
and the constant body produces antibodies

to kill them. Dozens of feet of coiled wiring
need to be teased out and snipped at the right spot,
and then, local anesthetic winding down, the doc

has to stuff it all back in like a flustered motorist
struggling to refold a road map. But never mind,
you'll fire blanks forever after. At first you may feel

peeled and solitary without your gang of unborn
children, so like the imaginary friends of childhood
and also like those alternate futures you'll never

live out and never relinquish because they're company,
and who'd blame you preferring company to love?
Most of the other animals live in groups we've named

so lavishly we must love them. Lions: a pride.
Foxes: a skulk. Larks: an exaltation. And geese:
a skein in the sky and a gaggle on the ground.

Venereal nouns, they're called, for the power Venus
had to provoke allegiances. But the future comes
by subtraction. The list dwindles of people

you'd rather be than you. Nobody in a dream
is dead, so when you wake at 5:00 A.M. to scuffle
across the hall and pee, to lower your umber line

and reel it back in dry, and then to lie back down
and bob like a moored boat two hours more,
you think how if you brought them all — the dead,

the living, the unborn — promiscuously on stage
as if for bows, what a pageant they'd make!
They would. They do. But by then you're back to sleep.

Selected Translations from the Bulgarian

(1991)

Vasil Sotirov
HUMAN HYMN

The slog of travelling it
makes your earthly path
dear beyond reckoning,
but if it comes to that
you'll push past the last
of it and into the beyond,

and there among the bushy
fig trees you'll pray
some Father of Ours
to give you for balm
in the gardens of Eden
the mirage of a desert.

Vasil Sotirov
YOU DANCE UP THERE

You dance just under the highest billow of the big top,
swathed in a gauzy white
like a light inside a cloud
or a recurring dream of one.

That your spirit sags
up there I understand
but you must, I pray
you, keep your body taut . . .

The downfall — that's what they come to see.
So do not fall, last
papery leaf
of my autumn:

dance instead,
oh dance

along the rope from which
I'm going to hang myself tomorrow . . .

Ussin Kerim
RECOLLECTIONS

What is he staring at, that waif,
who can he be, waiting for what?
The north wind snorts and batters
and nobody is safe.

Am I once more a child among children,
squinting into the grainy night
to see . . . what? My granny
brandishing a sooty lantern?

On the gnarled fingers of one hand
(forget the thumb) Granny can count
the peaceful days she's had,
and now I'm on the loose again.

"Where is he, that slither, that skulk,
that grandson of ours, do you know?
He's swarthy and he's pale
and wearing a tattered jacket."

Those deft games children play, where
have they fled and on what feet?
Why has the plaza emptied
and snow woven its nest in my hair?

And if I blunder into the river
and ride the chill flood where it goes,
who will saddle me with help,
or failing that, remember?

Ussin Kerim
UNTITLED POEM

> There's a slow fire in my eyes
> and a simmer at my heels.
> I want to be restless
> the rest of my life;
>
> to offer courtly greetings
> to the dogs who mark my path —
> a little bow, a tilted hat,
> some song I like to sing;
>
> to sleep unroofed in the woods,
> in the fields, to tell the rosary
> with stars instead of beads
> and break the day at dawn like bread;
>
> to wash my pale feet
> with a few tablespoons of dew
> and let my black hair extrude
> two sprigs of straw, or three;
>
> to pace and pace my country
> like a man confined to an infinite room;
> to stride through my life like a broom
> surely clearing a place to die.

Ussin Kerim
I LONG FOR A HORSE

> I long for a horse that can fly —
> hoofprints, hoofprints, and then none.
> Its mane is all I hold,
> and what's not us is sky.

I could watch my father hobble
through streets both of us loved.
I'd know him by his bald spot
and by the path he followed.

But none came out to welcome me
when I dreamt that I'd come back.
Our house was bleak. Likewise
the house across the street.

Granny Djina is dead
and Atta has married another man:
no wonder I took as a wife
and cure and job to the long road.

That cloud with its cargo of rain,
why ask where it goes next?
Oh heart why do you clatter
when you hear hooves again?

I long for a horse that can fly —
hoofprints, hoofprints, and then none.
Its mane is all I hold,
and what's not us is sky.

Ussin Kerim
BABAHAK

Dark gypsies have convened on the square
their carts and horses. Babahak, the dread
midsummer day, barbarous day
when the fathers sell their daughters here.

Demir and Alidjo wring and wring
their hands, reckoning, running
up each other's bids, and lithe Anifa
stands nearby, intent on not weeping.

And Meto, her beloved Meto, glowers
over there, his eyes shaded by rage
and pain. He's got a curved dagger
in his pocket and he'll wait for hours

if he must. Anifa's father
is urging a higher price: "Just look
at her, a very queen, a blessing
to the lucky man who'll have her.

She's worth five thousand at the least."
And the bids fly up like grackles.
"To buy this girl is to own a mill:
she'll turn and grind for you, and feed

you as long as you live." And Meto
fondles his curved dagger. He'll wait
for hours if he must, simmering
in the shadows. Meto has no

money and soon they will be shaking hands
and his great love is on the block.
Soon, very soon, any minute now,
Meto's curved dagger will flash

like furious lightning, and blood
will claim top bid for now.
But it's Babahak that should be riven,
if only the dagger could

cleave the tree and leave the stump to rot:
the venal fathers, the placid horses
lashing their tails at flies, the somnolent
squares, the smarmy handclasps. Babahak.

Ussin Kerim
MOTHER

Poor mother, my martyr,
you didn't get to raise your first-born son . . .
I ask the earth and the earth is mute:
where are you buried, Mother?

No trace, no place, no grave.
So when dusk falls my faithful
grief and I sit down to weep
like an old couple: at least we have

each other. I simmer with thirst
and day by day miss your warm hands.
My youth was washed away by a vile flood,
but this stone of grief endures.

I love to remember
playing with the other kids
and women whispering,
"He looks just like his mother."

Sometimes when black night had come
and I was launched on the white sea of dreams
you'd be there, alongside,
your steady hands, the salt, the foam.

You'd rock me in your lap,
you'd mop my tears with your lips,
and I'd subside from toss to lull,
as still as water in a cup.

I'd lay my head on your shoulder
and the earth would answer me,
though now you don't, though now you're mute,
though I still cry out, "Mother!"

from

Blues If You Want

(1989)

NABOKOV'S BLUES

The wallful of quoted passages from his work,
with the requisite specimens pinned next
to their literary cameo appearances, was too good

a temptation to resist, and if the curator couldn't,
why should we? The prose dipped and shimmered
and the "flies," as I heard a buff call them, stood

at lurid attention on their pins. If you love to read
and look, you could be happy a month in that small
room. One of the Nabokov photos I'd never seen:

he's writing (left-handed! why did I never trouble
to find out?) at his stand-up desk in the hotel
apartment in Montreux. The picture's mostly

of his back and the small wedge of face that shows
brims with indifference to anything not on the page.
The window's shut. A tiny lamp trails a veil of light

over the page, too far away for us to read.
We also liked the chest of specimen drawers
labeled, as if for apprentice Freudians,

"Genitalia," wherein languished in phials
the thousands he examined for his monograph
on the Lycaenidae, the silver-studded Blues.

And there in the center of the room a carillon
of Blues rang mutely out. There must have been
three hundred of them. Amanda's Blue was there,

and the Chalk Hill Blue, the Karner Blue
(*Lycaeides melissa samuelis* Nabokov),
a Violet-Tinged Copper, the Mourning Cloak,

an Echo Azure, the White-Lined Green Hairstreak,
the Cretan Argus (known only from Mt. Ida:
in the series Nabokov did on this beauty

he noted for each specimen the altitude at which
it had been taken), and as the ads and lovers say,
"and much, much more." The stilled belle of the tower

was a *Lycaeides melissa melissa*. No doubt
it's an accident Melissa rhymes, sort of, with Lolita.
The scant hour we could lavish on the Blues

flew by, and we improvised a path through cars
and slush and boot-high berms of mud-blurred snow
to wherever we went next. I must have been mute,

or whatever I said won from silence nothing
it mourned to lose. I was back in that small
room, vast by love of each flickering detail,

each genital dusting to nothing, the turn,
like a worm's or caterpillar's, of each phrase.
I stood up to my ankles in sludge pooled

over a stopped sewer grate and thought —
wouldn't you know it — about love and art:
you can be ruined ("rurnt," as we said in south-

western Ohio) by a book or improved by
a butterfly. You can dodder in the slop,
septic with a rage not for order but for the love

the senses bear for what they do, for the detail
that's never annexed, like a reluctant crumb
to a vacuum cleaner, to a coherence.

You can be bead after bead on perception's rosary.
This is the sweet ache that hurts most, the way
desire burns bluely at its phosphorescent core:

just as you're having what you wanted most,
you want it more and more until that's more
than you, or it, or both of you, can bear.

39,000 FEET

The cap'n never drawls, *We're seven miles*
or so above the earth and weigh more than
the town I grew up in. He says, *We've reached*
our cruising altitude. And how we labored
to get there. We held our armrests down lest
they career around the cabin and terrify
less experienced fliers, an acrid dew formed
on our palms, and none of us in coach
thought the word "steerage." There are certain
things the legal department has decreed
the cap'n must not say to an open microphone —
e.g., *Uh-oh* — for we have paid for tickets
and that means contract law, and these are
corporate lawyers, not the sorts who buy ad space
on matchbooks (Spinal Injury? Slither on in
to Tort, Writ and Blackmail for a free
consultation. *Hablamos español.*). Of course
if they'd done better at law school they wouldn't
work for an airline, they'd be free lances,
though "free" seems a strange word just there
indeed. Once in a hotel lobby in St. Louis
I overheard a celebrity lawyer spit into

a pay phone that he was sick and tired of all
the little people, and if cars look like ants
from a mile up imagine what we look like now —
a needle — if he could see us through the hotel
roof; his rage; the towering curds and paling wisps
of clouds; the blue, sourceless, amniotic light
in which the world, hidden by clouds, seems
from 39,000 feet to float. Drinks and then food
rumbled down the aisle. The cap'n came back
on the horn: *How do you like the flight so far?*
And lemme ask you all about that squall of baby
protest we rose through to level off. How
did you feel about it, and can you blame
the little imps? We couldn't. We were starting
our descent. Rich as we were in misgiving
when we took off, we liked the chill and lull
of 39,000 feet, for there we felt, I'm not sure
how to say this, somehow American. The law
seemed still a beautiful abstraction, and the land
we sped so far above was like the land we grew
up on, before the malls and apartment
complexes were named for what had been destroyed
to build them: Fair Meadows Mall, Tall Oaks
Townhouses. Trapped in the same experiment,
as ever, we turned to each other
our desperate American friendliness,
now our most spurned export, and rode
down, through tufts and tatters of clouds
and through *mild chop*, into Detroit, where
cap'n bade us good-bye and then the first-
class passengers *deplaned*, and then the rest
of us, some with imps and some without.

CHANGE OF ADDRESS

"It doesn't get much light," the real
estate agent allowed, and didn't say,
as Nora Joyce did of a flat James let,
"It's not a fit place to wash a rat in."

Figure a 50% divorce rate,
you've got one chance in two a sale
provokes another sale and maybe
two transactions after that,

a pyramid scheme for grief. The agent didn't
smirk, I'll hand her that. When I'm asleep
and my navel is like the calm bubble
in a carpenter's level, rage is safe,

the way animals in a zoo are safe,
a little skittish and depressed but safe,
and yes, a little off their feed but safe.
And the rat? The rat looks radiant.

IT DON'T MEAN A THING
IF IT AIN'T GOT THAT SWING

On the wine label, monks, towers and wimples.
The boy with damp hands and the girl with damp
panties. The spring air is a little drunk
on itself, after all, on its aftertaste of wet
pewter and on the flecks and spangles of light
it sifts through the shadows the oak leaves toss
this way and that, as though dealing cards.
A grackle unrolls like a carpet of sandpaper
its brash lament. A car with an ulcerated
muffler stutters past. Inside, the girl has on

those panties, the pale color of key lime pie,
and two comical earrings, one a rabbit,
one a carrot. He'd thought her body hair
might be darker, so that, let's say, the sluice
of hair from her navel to her pubic floss
would be like a file of ants showing
the way to a picnic, but it was pale
enough to catch, and to toss, the light. She's
all detail and all beautiful. So much to observe.
He hates being so inarticulate. He hates being
so inarticulate. First she removes the carrot,
then the rabbit. He bears them to the bedside table . . .

From what follows we turn away,
for we have manners
and our lovers need privacy to love
and talk and talk, for love is woven

from language
itself, from jokes, pet names and puns,
from anecdote, from double entendre
(already invaded by *tendre*), until

our lovers are a kind of literature
and sole mad scholiasts of it.
Inventors at Work, a sign on the bedroom
door might say.

It wasn't from the gods fire was stolen,
but from matter
(decay burning so steadily who'd think to speed
it up? It knew what it was doing). I think

it was language Prometheus got from the gods.
Isn't a tongue a flame? If I remember
the story right, he sailed
to the island of Lemnos, where Hephaestus

kept his forge, stole a brand of fire
and carried it back in a hollow stalk,
like smuggling music in a clarinet.
Who'd think to look

for it there? Who'd plan ahead to ask
Language how she'd fare far from gods?
She? For purposes of fable I've made her
a young woman.

She pined and waned,
she scuffled from kitchen to porch, she
sighed and each sigh seared its smoky
way from lung to mouth to the cornflower-

blue air toward which all spirit rose
and from which,
like logs collapsing in a fireplace, all
matter sank. This was long before writing;

Language was young and sad. She could
implore and charm, she could convince and scathe,
pick laughter's lock,
she could almost glow with her own powers,

but she was the wind's,
like jazz before recordings. Deep into
the pockets of her smock she thrust her fists.
She stamped a comely foot (and on one ankle bone,

it's worth mentioning, she bore the tattoo
of a butterfly —
Nabokov's Blue, unless I miss my guess,
O.D., F. Martin Brown, 1955), she raised

a quizzical shoulder and let sag languidly
a pout.
Oh, I'd give anything, she cried,
if I could be memorable.

Anything?
intoned the opportunistic devil from
behind a papier-mâché boulder. *Yes,
anything*, she said, and thus the deal

was struck, and writing was invented.
But to be written down she gave up
pout, toss, crinkle,
stamp and shrug, shiver, flout and pucker,

the long, cunning lexicon of the body,
and thus what we lazily call "form"
in poetry,
let's say, is Language's desperate

attempt to wrench from print
the voluble body it gave away
in order to be read.
(By the way, my sweet, I think you'll

recognize "between the lines" —
talk about form! —
not the generic "young woman,"
nor Eve nor muse nor other bimbo,

but 100 lb. you, smoldering demurely
under one of your ravishing hats
like a brand in a hollow stalk, let's
say, on a twilit porch . . .)

Where was I? Oh yes, our lovers. Which ones?
Ha ha. We'll not eavesdrop, but if we did we'd
hear them murmuring. Those aren't sweet nothings,
they're the very dial tone love's open line makes.
Even the gruff swain in the neighboring car
that night at the Montgomery Drive-In thirty
years ago, in panic as mute love spread through
his body like a willful shapelessness, went to work.

I love you baby (two-beat pause), *no shit.*
When you're so terrified you call a beloved
institution like the Montgomery Drive-In
"the finger bowl," and we all did, you've a long
way to go and his cry was a fine beginning.
A snowflake sizzles against the window of my
hotel room. Ann Arbor, late at night. My bonnie
lies not over the ocean but over a Great Lake
or two. Now I lay me down to sleep, I used
to say, the first great poem I knew by heart.
Could I but find the words and lilt, there's some-
thing I'd tell you, sweetie. I don't know what
it is, but I'm on the case, let me tell you,
the way convicts can tell you all about the law.

HOUSECOOLING

Those ashes shimmering dully in the fireplace,
like tarnished fish scales? I swept them out.
Those tiny tumbleweeds of dust that stalled
against a penny or a paperclip under the bed?
I lay along the grain of the floorboards
and stared each pill into the vacuum's mouth.
I loved that house and I was moving out.

What do you want to do when you grow up?
they asked, and I never said, *I want to haunt
a house.* But I grew pale. The way the cops "lift"
fingerprints, that's how I touched the house.
The way one of my sons would stand in front
of me and say, *I'm outta here*, and he would mean
it, his crisp, heart-creasing husk delivering

a kind of telegram from wherever the rest of him
had gone — that's how I laved and scoured
and patrolled the house, and how I made my small

withdrawals and made my wan way outta there.
And then I was gone. I took what I could.
Each smudge I left, each slur, each whorl, I left
for love, but love of what I cannot say.

HOMER'S SEEING-EYE DOG

Most of the time he wrote, a sort of sleep
with a purpose, so far as I could tell.
How he got from the dark of sleep
to the dark of waking up I'll never know;
the lax sprawl sleep allowed him
began to set from the edges in,
like a custard, and then he was awake —
me too, of course, wriggling my ears
while he unlocked his bladder and stream
of dopey wake-up jokes. The one
about the wine-dark pee I hated instantly.
I stood at the ready, like a god
in an epic, but there was never much
to do. Oh, now and then I'd make a sure
intervention, save a life, whatever.
But my exploits don't interest you,
and of his life all I can say is that
when he'd poured out his work
the best of it was gone and then he died.
He was a great man and I loved him.
Not a whimper about his sex life —
how I detest your prurience —
but here's a farewell literary tip:
I myself am the model for Penelope.
Don't snicker, you hairless moron,
I know so well what "faithful" means
there's not even a word for it in Dog.
I just embody it. I think you bipeds
have a catch phrase for it: "To thine own self

be true, . . ." though like a blind man's shadow,
the second half is only there for those who know
it's missing. Merely a dog, I'll tell you
what it is: ". . . as if you had a choice."

THE BLUES

What did I think, a storm clutching a clarinet
and boarding a downtown bus, headed for lessons?
I had pieces to learn by heart, but at twelve

you think the heart and memory are different.
" 'It's a poor sort of memory that only works
backwards,' the Queen remarked." *Alice in Wonderland.*

Although I knew the way music can fill a room,
even with loneliness, which is of course a kind
of company. I could swelter through an August

afternoon — torpor rising from the river — and listen
to J. J. Johnson and Stan Getz braid variations
on "My Funny Valentine," and feel there in the room

with me the force and weight of what I couldn't
say. What's an emotion anyhow?
Lassitude and sweat lay all around me

like a stubble field, it was so hot and listless,
but I was quick and furtive like a fox
who has thirty miles a day metabolism

to burn off as ordinary business.
I had about me, after all, the bare eloquence
of the becalmed, the plain speech of the leafless

tree. I had the cunning of my body and a few
bars — they were enough — of music. Looking back,
it almost seems as though I could remember —

but this can't be; how could I bear it? —
the future toward which I'd clatter
with that boy tied like a bell around my throat,

a brave man and a coward both,
to break and break my metronomic heart
and just enough to learn to love the blues.

MOONLIGHT IN VERMONT

It's the very end of summer
and one night, probably this week, frost will sear,
like dry ice, a few leaves on trees that forayed
a few feet from the huddle of the woods, and there

they'll be, come morning, waving their red hands
like proud culprits.
One year mosquitoes clung to and trailed from
the walls and ceilings thick as tatty fabric,

and another rain lambasted us derisively
until the sogged lawns steeped like rice
in paddies. But each
year there's a dusk when the moon, like tonight's,

has risen early and every hue and tint of blue
creeps out, like an audience come to music,
to be warmed by the moon's pale fire. A car
or truck whisks

by on 125.
Somebody's hurrying home, I suppose.
Each blue is lined with a deeper blue, the way
an old magician's sleeves might be composed

of handkerchiefs. There's no illusion here.
It's beautiful to watch
and that's reason enough for blue after blue
to blossom, for each decaying swatch

to die into the next. The faster it goes
the less hurry I'm in for home or anywhere.
Like a vast grape the full
moon hangs above an empty Adirondack chair.

By now the moon itself is blue. By this
we mean that we can see in it the full freight
of our unspent love for it, for the blue night,
and for the hour, which is late.

EVERY TUB

The way some of us played cards and some drank
and some of us ran the tiny motors of talk long
into the night — so many needs and habits, don't
you know? — you'd think there'd have been at least
one of us awake at any hour of the night, but then
sometimes I'd wake at dawn and miss the idle
hum that we give off when we're awake and know
as steadily as the bus droned on and sleep
drained out of me, I and the driver were the only
ones awake. Even the boss, who used to sit
like a night-light directly back of the driver,
where we couldn't see him in the rearview mirror,
had withdrawn his interest in the world.
Once in northern Oklahoma I saw a sunrise
I'd take to the grave with me if there were room.
It came out of the dark like ground fog, gray
at first, and then metallic pink soaked through
the gray as if a blotter were being saturated
from beneath, and all this time the sun itself
was under the horizon's rim. Then it was orange

and then, as if in triumph and escape,
it spun up at me like a balloon of blood
and in five minutes the sky was stained
a sweet blue every way I looked. It's as hard
to describe now as it was to look at then,
you've got to pay such fierce attention. See,
the reason I'm a musician is, Language and I,
we love each other but we never got it on,
so as the saying goes, we're just good friends,
though I surely love to talk. So now it's thirty
minutes after dawn and the guys are waking up.
Their voices are furred by sleep and their joints
grate from sleeping sitting up. Next thing
you know the driver blows a turn and we're far
from the highway, blundered into a pouch
of splendid houses warmed by rich people
sleeping. Now everyone's awake, and the bus
is rife with cries. "Dig it, that house is *my* house."
"Look to your left and right, my man, we've
discovered America." Stuff like that. Then Bo
says with that I'm-crossing-the-street-don't-
vex-me-with-your-stoplights tone in his voice,
"You wrong about America, you have to get in line
to say so. This bus is America." This bus?
I looked around the bus and saw my world,
and smelled the chicken and whiskey and pride
and unchanged socks and bitter jokes.
"This bus don't stop till we're happy," said Bo.
He flicked a dismissive wrist at the sleeping rich:
"They quit." I guess I don't need to tell you
we didn't. I spent thirty-six years on the road
and that dawn I was twenty-four. The driver
sniffed us out of there and on our way.
We got in two P.M. or so with no gig until eight.
The boss meant business but he meant pleasure,
too. Maybe you know the way he told us we were
on our own till eight? "Every tub on its own base."

School Days

Once those fences kept me in. Mr. Mote
threw a dictionary at me in that room
on the corner, second floor, he and I
hypnotized by spite and everyone else
docile by default, for all we had was

fourth-grade manners: two gasped,
three tittered, Laneta hid her lovely head,
six palely watched their shoes as if they'd
brim and then flood urine, and the rest . . .
Good God, I'd forgot the rest. It's been

thirty-some years. That smart-ass afternoon
I loved them all and today all I can remember
is the name of one I loved and one I hated.
Wasn't he right to hurl at me a box
of words? By the time the dictionary spun

to rest under the radiator, its every page
was blank and the silent room was strewn
with print. I can't remember how we found
something to do, to bore up through that pall.
It would be as hard as that to remember

all their names — though, come to think of it,
I can. Isn't that how I got here,
and with you? I'm going to start at the north-
east corner of that hallucinated room
and name them one by one and row by row.

A phalanx of cabs surges uptown in tune
to the staggered lights and two young black
men spurt across the dark avenue (two A.M.)

ahead of them: *We're here, motherfuckers,*
don't mess up. Three of five cabs honk: *We're here*
too, older and clawing for a living, don't

fuck up. The cabs rush uptown and the lights
go green ahead like a good explanation.
Everyone knows this ballet. Nobody falls or brakes.

Tonight I talked for hours and never said
one thing so close to the truculent heart of speech
as those horn blats, that dash across Amsterdam,

not to persuade nor to be understood but
a kind of signature, a scrawl on the air:
We're here, room for all of us if we be alert.

LITTLE BLUE NUDE

Outside, the crackhead who panhandles an eight-
hour-day at 106th and Broadway croons
for Earl, his man, to let him in and make him well.
Soon the super's son will take his triumvirate

of dogs across the street to crap in Central Park.
Through my wall I'll hear the scrabble of their claws
and the low whirl of near-barks in their throats
as they tug their leashes down the hall and out

the door. The night a burglar forced the gate
across my kitchen window and slithered in to clean
me out, those dogs slept next door like drunken clouds.
I was in Tennessee. When I got off the plane there,

my host glanced at my tiny bag and asked, "Those
all your worldly goods?" I know you didn't ask me
what they took, but you can guess you're going to hear
the list. People tell these stories until they've worn

them out. A TV and a tape deck, two phones,
an answering machine, an alarm clock that didn't
work — these you'd expect, for they can be most
easily swept, like flecks of silt, into the swift

currents of the River Fence. The anomalies
make such lists interesting. These were mine:
two sets of sheets and pillowcases, and a bottle
of Côte Roti, 1982. Now these were clues. Also

he left my typewriter. And I knew right away
who'd robbed me. The mere pressure of my key
in the lock, before I'd even turned it, swung my door
open and my body knew he'd come in through

the kitchen but left like a guest by the front door.
Tony, my dumpster-diving friend, would bring by
things to sell: a ream of letterhead stationery
from The Children's Aid Society and two half

gallons of orange juice. Three dollars. "Whoo," he'd say.
"Ain't it a wonder what people will throw out."
So you see I was a sort of fence myself. "Being
a writer, you could probably use some paper"

was the way he'd introduced himself. The night
before I left for Tennessee he'd pasted his girlfriend
Shirley in the eye and she came by my apartment
to complain. I gave her some ice cubes nested

in a kitchen towel to hold against her bruise,
and a glass of wine. So that explains the Côte Roti.
As for the sheets, when I confronted Tony,
he yelled at me, "A dick don't have no conscience."

Speak for yourself, I thought redundantly, for I'm
the one with the typewriter and gall to speak
for others. Tony's his only clientele. "I didn't rob
your place," he yelled, "and stay away from Shirley."

The wonder is how much we manage to hang on to.
Even if a robbery's been designed to hurt,
no thief would know to take the postcard
of Renoir's *Little Blue Nude* I'd taped above my desk.

She sits, all wist and inner weather on her creamy
skin, her face bemused beneath the ginger helmet
of her hair, wholly alert to what the poets once
called reverie, perhaps, though from the relaxed

attention of her body I'd say she was listening
to beloved music. If I could choose for her,
I'd make it Ellington's 1940 recording
of "Cottontail," with Ben Webster on tenor.

If you'd been robbed, let's say, and rage ran through
you like a wind, and you balled your fists and sat
and stared at them, as though you'd forget their name,
you who are so good with words, rehearsing irate

speeches for Tony, wrapped in fury like a flower
in a bud; and also feeling impotent, a chump
with a mouthful of rant, a chump who knows
even now he'll eat the rage, the loss, the sour

tang of moral superiority to Tony,
the times he'll tell the story and list what Tony
stole . . . If you could see all those words coming
and know even now you'd eat them, every one,

you could turn to music you love, not as a mood-
altering drug nor as a consolation, but because
your emotions had overwhelmed and tired you
and made you mute and stupid, and you rued

them every one. But when Webster kicks into
his first chorus, they're back, all your emotions,
every one, and in another language, perhaps
closer to their own. "There you are," you say

to them silently, and you're vivid again, the way
we're most ourselves when we know surely
what we love, and whom. The little blue nude
has a look on her face like that. Once

when I was fussing with my tapes, Tony came by
to sell me mineral water and envelopes.
"You writing a book on jazz or what?" "No,"
I said, "I just love these." I didn't say why,

because I didn't talk that way to Tony,
and because, come to think of it, I didn't know
that day, I didn't ask myself until later,
afterthought being the writer's specialty

and curse. But that conversation explains why
he took the tapes and left the typewriter.
Writing's my scam, he thought, and music my love.
The dogs come snuffling and scrabbling back.

This time of night the building quiets down,
the hour of soliloquists. Even with walls this thin
the neighbors don't complain when I type late.
"Still working on that book?" they ask.

"What's it about?" one asked. I didn't know
that day, I didn't ask myself until later.
It's a reverie on what I love, and whom,
and how I manage to hold on to them.

Onions

How easily happiness begins by
dicing onions. A lump of sweet butter
slithers and swirls across the floor
of the sauté pan, especially if its
errant path crosses a tiny slick
of olive oil. Then a tumble of onions.

This could mean soup or risotto
or chutney (from the Sanskrit
chatni, to lick). Slowly the onions
go limp and then nacreous
and then what cookbooks call clear,
though if they were eyes you could see

clearly the cataracts in them.
It's true it can make you weep
to peel them, to unfurl and to tease
from the taut ball first the brittle,
caramel-colored and decrepit
papery outside layer, the least

recent the reticent onion
wrapped around its growing body,
for there's nothing to an onion
but skin, and it's true you can go on
weeping as you go on in, through
the moist middle skins, the sweetest

and thickest, and you can go on
in to the core, to the bud-like,
acrid, fibrous skins densely
clustered there, stalky and in-
complete, and these are the most
pungent, like the nuggets of nightmare

and rage and murmury animal
comfort that infant humans secrete.
This is the best domestic perfume.
You sit down to eat with a rumor
of onions still on your twice-washed
hands and lift to your mouth a hint

of a story about loam and usual
endurance. It's there when you clean up
and rinse the wine glasses and make
a joke, and you leave the minutest
whiff of it on the light switch,
later, when you climb the stairs.

STRAIGHT LIFE

There's grit in the road, and pumice,
and grease in which too many stale fish
have been fried. There are twists of breadcrust
with flourishing settlements of grey-blue
and iridescent green, and there's a wedding
band a hurt woman flung from a taxi window.
There's loneliness richer than topsoil
in Iowa, and there are swales and hollows
of boredom that go by as if trundled
by stagehands, unloved and worse,
unnoticed. Scenery, we call it, and land-
scape, when boredom is on us like a caul.
The bells of cats dead so long their names
have been forgot are bulldozed into the road,
and tendrils of rusting chrome and flecks
of car paint with ambitious names —
British Racing Green and *Claret.*
Cinders and tar and sweat and tax hikes
and long-term bonds. Like a village

at the base of an active volcano,
the road is built of its history.
It's we who forget, who erred and swerved
and wandered and drove back and forth
and seemed aimless as teenagers,
though one of us steered the whole time.

The way it happened, see, we played in Dallas,
the state fair, for some black dance. Cat with a beautiful
white suit, Palm Beach maybe, dancing his ass
off. You look up from the charts, you see that white suit
like a banner in the center of the floor. Next thing
you know there's a big circle of people moving
back, the way you throw a rock in water and it broadcasts
rings and rings, moving back. You travel
and you travel, some things you don't forget.
Two cats in the center, one of them the cat in the white
suit and suddenly the suit was soaked-through red.

Coleman Hawkins used to say he'd been born
on a ship, in no country at all, though I think
he said it to remind himself how torn he felt
between being American at heart and the way
Europeans treated black musicians. This life,
it's easy to feel you've been born on the road.
You know the fine coat of dust furniture grows
just standing there? We grow it traveling.
We're on the road and the road's on us.
I used to ask myself each morning where I was
but slowly learned to know — and this is how
you tell a man who's traveled some and paid
attention — by looking at the sky. A sky's
a fingerprint. All along the road the food's
the same and no two beds you hang your toes
over the end of are. That's when you've got
a bed. Some nights we just pulled the bus
off the road like a docked boat. After some towns
there'd be a scatter of spent condoms

where we'd parked, the way in a different life
you throw coins in a fountain, to come back
or not, whichever seemed the better luck.

I loved her earlobes and her niblet toes
and how the crook of her elbow smelled.
I loved one of her fingers most but a new
one every day. I loved how at the onset
of desire her eyes would go a little milky
the way water does just before the surface
of it shimmers when it starts to boil.
Telling how much I loved her made me talk
as well as I can play. One time she told me
what Dame Nellie Melba said: *There's only
two things I like stiff, and one of them is Jell-O.*
Then she let loose a laugh like a dropped
drawer of silverware. Here's what I said:
*I love every juice and tuft and muscle
of you, honey, each nub and bog and fen,
each prospect and each view.* That's what
I like to say I said, though where'd I learn
to talk like that? Same place I learned to play.
You know how people always ask each other
How you feel? You learn to look straight
at the answer without flinching, then spend
ten years to learn your instrument.
Good luck helps, too. Of course somewhere along
that line I let my sweetie slip away. Truth is,
that was by choice. But I was with her
when I learned how some things can't be fully
felt until they're said. Including this salute.

You shuffle into some dingebox and there's
an audience of six, three of them sober.
The chill fire of its name in neon bathes
the windows. In the mist outside, the stoplights
are hazy and big, like lazy memories of pleasure,
and as they change in their languorous sequence,

going green and going downtown, an explanation
beckons, but of what? Too late, it's gone. No use
in staring moodily out the window.
Whatever it is, it will be back. Tires slur
on the rainy pavement outside. You've never
looked into a mirror to watch the next thing
you do, but it would identify you to yourself
faster than anything you know. You can remember it,
and in advance, with a sure and casual
rapacity. You duck your left shoulder a little
and sweep your tongue in a slight crescent
first under your top lip, then over the bottom.
You lay a thin slather on the reed and take
on a few bars of breath. Emily Dickinson
wrote of Judge Otis Philips Lord that *Abstinence
from Melody was what made him die.*
Music's only secret is silence. It's time
to play, time to tell whatever you know.

A RED SILK BLOUSE

So much for taupe and beige and eggshell,
for ecru (is that an ungulate?), for bone,
for teal (is that something the rich shoot?),
for burgundy, navy and champagne. Let's market

a smear of new colors: rust, infantry, menstrual
blood, chalkdust and liverspots, colicky vomit.
So much for the women-and-children-last
politics of clothing, and so much for black shoes.

If cheap-seaside-summer-rental mildew
is too murky a color to sell, even in silk
with its slubs where the slathering worms
double-clutched, let's show a line based

on the lurid, neon, garish tropical
fish, on the third world of colors. Let's drape
your creamy torso slowly in red and slowly un-
veil it. At long last we're in business.

Mood Indigo

From the porch; from the hayrick where her prickled
brothers hid and chortled and slurped into their young pink
lungs the ash-blond dusty air that lay above the bales

like low clouds; and from the squeak and suck
of the well-pump and from the glove of rust it implied
on her hand; from the dress parade of clothes

in her mothproofed closet; from her tiny Philco
with its cracked speaker and Sunday litany
(*Nick Carter, The Shadow, The Green Hornet, Sky King*);

from the loosening bud of her body; from hunger,
as they say, and from reading; from the finger
she used to dial her own number; from the dark

loam of the harrowed fields and from the very sky;
it came from everywhere. Which is to say it was
always there, and that it came from nowhere.

It evaporated with the dew, and at dusk when dark
spread in the sky like water in a blotter, it spread, too,
but it came back and curdled with milk and stung

with nettles. It was in the bleat of the lamb, the way
a clapper is in a bell, and in the raucous, scratchy
gossip of the crows. It walked with her to school and lay

with her to sleep and at last she was well pleased.
If she were to sew, she would prick her finger with it.
If she were to bake, it would linger in the kitchen

like an odor snarled in the deepest folds of childhood.
It became her dead pet, her lost love, the baby sister
blue and dead at birth, the chill headwaters of the river

that purled and meandered and ran and ran until
it issued into her, as into a sea, and then she was its
and it was wholly hers. She kept to her room, as we

learned to say, but now and then she'd come down
and pass through the kitchen, and the screen door
would close behind her with no more sound than

an envelope being sealed, and she'd walk for hours
in the fields like a lithe blue rain, and end up
in the barn, and one of us would go and bring her in.

Index of Titles and First Lines

Titles are set in italic type.

William Matthews was born in Cincinnati, Ohio, in 1942, and was educated at Yale University (B.A.) and the University of North Carolina at Chapel Hill (M.A.). He is professor of English at the City College of the City University of New York. At various times he has been president of Associated Writing Programs and of the Poetry Society of America, and he has been on the literature panel of the National Endowment for the Arts, serving briefly as its chairman. He lives in New York City.